Poking Holes *in the* Darkness

by

Jaki Parlier

Poking Holes in the Darkness

P.O. Box 628200
Orlando, FL 32862-8200

Cover design by Tanya Parlier
Photography by Jim Parlier
Inside artwork by Don Drew Canonge

First printing © 1994, published by Promise Publishing Co.

Printed in the United States of America

ISBN 0-938978-24-1

Visit Wycliffe's Web Site at www.wycliffe.org

Dedication

Dedicated with love to my husband,

Jim,

whose work among the Managalasi people, and the life he lived before them, demonstrated to me the true meaning of the word steadfast. Because of his unending patience and unwavering belief in what the Lord can accomplish, I have learned to walk more by faith and less by sight.

Contents

Foreword

Heaven was stunned in silence. Angels didn't know what to say. The moment anticipated since before the foundation of earth had finally come. The Father and the Son, who had never spent a day or night apart, were saying good-bye. He was leaving all the indescribable comforts of heaven for all the undeniable pains of earth. He who was 100 percent God was about to become 100 percent human. In the words of Jesus' biographer, "the Word became flesh and made his dwelling among us" (John 1:14).

It was an incredible sacrifice for God's only Son to become like us, to be called Jesus, to settle for our simple ways, to learn our culture and speak our language, and for "him who had no sin to be sin for us, so that we in him might become the righteousness of God" (2 Corinthians 5:21).

It was very hard. It was very good. It was the incarnation.

When I was a boy, I met two people very much like Jesus. Jim and Judy Parlier answered the same call God gave His Son. They agreed to say good-bye to their lifelong homeland in order to dwell among the Managalasi people in Papua New Guinea, to become like them in order to love them, to learn their ways, to speak their language—so that the Managalasi could know God, follow Jesus and live forever.

It was very hard. It was very good. It was incarnational one more time. Some say it was an incredible sacrifice.

I say: it was just like Jesus.

Leith Anderson
Wooddale Church
Eden Prairie, Minnesota

Acknowledgments

Happily, I give my deepest thanks to two very special people, Martha Norris and Kim Beaty, my cheering squad, for their encouragement and invaluable editing help in the shaping of this book.

I am indebted to Shirl Thomas, who (although she never met me) offered her help. Thank you, Shirl, for smoothing out the wrinkles in my final manuscript.

Thanks are also due to Nancy Duncan, Debbie Dierks, Elona Siemsen, Randy Parlier, Betty Asmuth and Frankie Jackson for their suggestions and for their help with proofreading.

Section One

The Incredible Sacrifice

The Incredible Sacrifice

Departing Ukarumpa, our center of operations in Papua New Guinea, Jim and I soared over the dragon-shaped island in a single engine aircraft. We were on the way to begin our lives with the Managalasi people. Jim had already visited once and made arrangements through an interpreter to live on a piece of their land. Before he left, some men from a village called "Numba" promised to gather wood and poles for our house.

The Managalasis lived east of Port Moresby, the nation's capital, and had never heard the Gospel. Nor did they have one verse of Scripture in their language. It was up to us, Jim and me, to translate the New Testament into their language and help them learn about Jesus.

As we flew over mountains and valleys that stretched from horizon to horizon, I felt excitement mounting within me. All of our training—Bible school, medical school and linguistics—was behind us. We were beginning a new chapter of our lives,

Mountains loomed, stretching from horizon to horizon.

the chapter that would bring about the fulfillment of our training and the purpose for which we were born. My heart raced inside me.

I leaned back in my seat and closed my eyes. How vividly I remembered that fateful day in November, 1959, when I rode the trolley car to Bamberger's Department Store in Newark, New Jersey.

Shivering beneath my heavy coat and woolen scarf, I squeezed into the elevator with other Bamberger employees and pressed number nine. Unenthusiastic eyes stared vacantly into space as if life held nothing exciting for them.

The elevator doors slid open revealing a large room with desks in every available space. Promising young executives trained here hoping to move up with Bamberger and Company—a leading department store in New Jersey. Fresh out of Bible school, I worked as secretary to three junior executives.

I headed for the locker room which also served as the break room. Gray steel lockers and dark furniture added a chill to the windowless room. After cramming my coat into the narrow locker, I spun around too quickly and nearly collided with Miss Lucinda, my supervisor.

Lucinda Shipley appeared to be in her early forties. Her short hair was as black as her eyes, both of which offset a banana-shaped nose much too long for her face.

"Good morning, Mrs. Parlier," she said perfunctorily, removing her chic, brown fur.

"Good morning," I mumbled, intimidated by her superiority, then hurried to begin work. But the "Mrs." part brought a smile to my lips. Jim and I had been married only five months, and being called "Mrs. Parlier" still thrilled me.

The mail sat on my desk in a large, canvas bag, ready to be distributed or re-routed. After a few minutes I looked up and caught Miss Lucinda's cold, hard glare. *Why is she looking at me like that?* I wondered, and shifted uneasily in my chair. My hands shook as I reached for another piece of mail. As I watched the slender figure move to the other side of the room, I breathed a sigh of relief.

At ten o'clock I poured myself a cup of coffee and sat down on a folding chair in the break room. Then Miss Lucinda entered and headed for the coffee pot. A band of pressure seemed to tighten around my chest. I tried not to stare at the expensive, powder blue knit dress that clung to her slim figure. She sat down across from me and crossed one well-shaped leg over the other. The blue shoe dangling from her foot was the same shade as her dress. Matching beads and earrings created a shimmering azure effect that sparked life in the dreary room.

Co-workers filtered in and sat down to smoke. They flipped through magazines as if totally bored. My eyes wandered to the vision in blue and met her gaze head-on. Feeling that I should say something, I blurted out: "I like your outfit."

"Thank you," she replied. "Powder blue is my favorite color. Everything I'm wearing today matches from my dress down to my skin."

"Really?" I exclaimed, genuinely amazed.

"Oh yes. My panties are blue, my corset is blue, my bra and slip are blue." At the last she lifted up the hem of her dress, revealing several inches of light blue lace at the bottom of a silky, blue slip.

"How beautiful!" I exclaimed with open admiration.

"Oh I wear matching undergarments every day," she added. "If I wear a beige dress, I wear beige down to my skin. When I wear purple, all my undergarments are purple. I just wouldn't feel right if everything didn't match."

She uncrossed her leg and stretched it straight out in front of her. "Look at this," she pointed out, "even my stockings are blue! It may be hard to tell, but they're blue."

Sure enough, the smooth stockings were tinged with the most subtle shade of blue. I swung my leg out to contrast shades and then gasped at the sight of a thick run extending from ankle to knee. Instantly I drew my leg back and stood up fumbling with my coffee cup. "I'd better get back to work," I muttered and hurried for the door, but her next words stopped me dead in my tracks.

"So, I hear you're going to be a missionary," she said aloud. Every head turned my way.

"Yes," I admitted, looking into fiery eyes. Was that glint of anger intended for me, or was I imagining it? "My husband and I are going to Papua New Guinea to translate the Bible."

"New Guinea!" She spit out the words. "What a horrible place to live! When are you going?"

"As soon as we have enough money for passage—next year sometime." I glanced at the others in the room. The women had abandoned their magazines and sat listening to our conversation. I felt like a performer on stage.

"Do you and your husband intend to have children?" The edge in my supervisor's voice set my hands to shaking again.

"Well, er, yes. I think so."

"You **think** so? Don't you **know**?" The blue eye makeup became a blur, and the hawk-like nose seemed larger than life. I opened my mouth but no words came.

"And what about the grandparents? Will you deprive them of seeing their grandchildren?"

I was on trial now, fighting to save our future. "Well," I began, and hesitated, knowing how foolish this would sound. "Every five years we'll come back to the States for a furlough."

"What kind of schools do they have in the jungle?"

"I don't know," I admitted weakly. "We'll have to send them away to school...somewhere...I suppose."

"Well, then," she concluded, taking full advantage of my ignorance, "why are you going to deprive your children of all America has to offer? Isn't that an incredible sacrifice to make for heathen people?"

Eyes like two black coals burned into me from her petite, exquisite form. I wanted to disappear, yet I was unable to look away from the distorted face.

My voice emerged in barely a whisper. "God...God told us to go and give the Gospel to all the nations." I was painfully aware my statement sounded absurd to this unchurched woman.

"Those people have their own religion!" She was on the edge of her chair now. "They're happy as they are—why do you want to change them?"

"Because there's only one way to heaven, and we want those people to know the Truth."

"But you don't really care about what the natives want, or what's best for your children. You only care about your church work. You're selfish people! That's what I hate about missionaries!"

A smear of blue colors rose from the chair and, with brisk, deliberate steps, Miss Lucinda stalked from the room. With a sinking sensation, I knew that somewhere I had missed the mark and failed God miserably.

Now, through the window, I observed water gushing from the sides of the mountains, splashing at the bottom with a powerful spray, then forking into snakelike rivers that slithered through the jungle below.

Water gushed from mountainsides forming snakelike rivers that slithered through the jungle.

Jim sat in front next to our pilot, James Vincent Baptista, and tried to carry on a conversation over the roar of the engine. James looked back at me and yelled, "That's Mount Lamington! It blew up in 1951 and killed hundreds of people."

I looked at the smoking volcano, bold and sinister beneath the sun, and tried to imagine the hordes of people at its base running for their lives. A shiver of horror swept through my body. "Why is it still smoking?" I yelled back.

"It's always smoking," he said. "A lot of those people died right in their village, smothered from ash in the steam."

James read educational books, encyclopedias and magazines like *National Geographic* in his spare time. He retained information on many subjects, and whenever we visited the Baptista home at Ukarumpa, I enjoyed learning from him.

"Don't worry," James continued, "the Managalasis live three mountain ridges away, too far to be affected." I knew James had read everything in print concerning Papua New Guinea. There wasn't much about the country he didn't know.

"Is your seat belt fastened?" he asked, and I nodded. "We should be landing in another ten minutes."

Immediately I leaned forward and scanned the landscape for an airstrip. A few minutes passed, and I spotted a patch of brown, carved in the midst of twisted jungle foliage.

Sila Airstrip spread out on the side of a hill like a patch carved out of jungle foliage.

As we got closer, James made a slow circle over the strip. I saw Managalasis streaming out from beneath the brush to crowd around the edge of the airstrip. Moments later the plane landed, back wheels touching down first.

The Cessna sounded like a creaky old rocking chair as we bumped and swerved to the top of the incline. Hundreds of Managalasis dressed in painted bark cloth surrounded the plane, trying to peer inside. Jim hopped out first and swung the door open for me to jump down. As soon as my feet hit the ground, hordes of women engulfed me.

"Ese!" they said, touching my hair, feeling the fabric of my dress and patting my face. "Ese, ese!"

It must be their word for "welcome," I reasoned, and repeated the word back to them. The women shouted excitedly to one another with enormous smiles, as if I could already speak their language. Their eyes danced, and the happy smiles displayed reddish-black teeth. I caught my breath. Then a thin, middle-aged woman spit out a blob of the red mixture she had been swishing in her mouth. She wiped her lips with her forearm. "Ese!" she said, reaching out to shake my hand. I took her hand in mine and gazed down at the red blob on the grass. It had the consistency of chewing tobacco stained with a deep purple-red color. *What is that awful red stuff they're chewing?* I wondered.

It seemed as if the eyes of every woman and child were on me, waiting to hear me say more. Unnerved, I looked around for Jim. He and James were removing boxes from the plane.

Jim happened to turn my way and seeing my discomfort, called out, "You're the first American woman they've ever seen! They want to inspect you to see if you're like them. You don't have to say anything. Just smile!"

I looked back at the dark, strange faces and repeated "ese" over and over. The smile felt plastered to my face. I didn't know how long I could keep this up.

Looking around, I caught a glimpse of a child, two or three years old, peering at me from beneath long eyelashes. I reached out with both arms, and she screamed as if being attacked by a vicious animal. I felt so foreign, so strange. While the child's mother tried to shush her, I seized the opportunity as an excuse to leave the group and join Jim.

"What's that red stuff the women are chewing?" I asked him.

"Betelnut," Jim replied as he and James Vincent hoisted the 44-gallon drum packed with our belongings out of the plane. Then Jim gestured upward with his chin. "There's some betelnut growing over there on that tree."

I turned and gazed upward at a tree that resembled a date palm. Bright, grass-green nuts, the size of walnuts, hung down on a stalk. *How could something so nauseating be the product of such a beautiful palm tree?* I wondered.

Then, all too soon, it was time for James Vincent to return to Ukarumpa.

"Well, I'll see you in about six months," he said and climbed into the plane. I swallowed the lump forming in my throat and looked around at the mass of people, all exclaiming in a language I did not understand. My heart felt like lead inside my chest.

Men wearing loincloths of bark yelled at the women, who scooped up children from the plane's path and scurried into the brush. The strangeness of a totally new culture grabbed me. Instantly, I became aware of trading my comfortable, modern way of life for an isolated, stone-age culture.

The engine started up and I watched the plane taxi to the top of the field and turn around. Suddenly I had only one consuming desire—to get back into the Cessna with the pilot and leave this place. *Don't go!* My heart cried. *Don't go without me!* I tried to control my emotions, lest I rush out to the aircraft and pound on the door, begging to be let back in.

With a quick wave, James roared down the strip and was airborne in seconds.

Come back! Don't leave me here! I cried inside as the Cessna climbed into the sky. I bit down hard on my lip to keep the tears in check. Standing motionless, I watched the retreating Cessna till it became the size of a black crow. Some younger girls looked my way and giggled. *Do they see the pain mirrored on my face? What else would they be laughing at?*

All at once, I wanted Mom—my best friend. I longed to sit with her at the kitchen table drinking coffee. Thoughts of not seeing Mom for five years brought scalding tears to my eyes.

I don't want to stay here, I admitted to myself. *I have no desire to live with these strangers. I must have been crazy to come, completely out of my head. I'll never learn their language. I just want to go home.*

Then I took a good look at the Managalasi people—my new family. In that moment I realized that a hundred years of training could not have prepared me for this moment. *No,* I said to myself. *These people will never be "family" to me. Never!*

The brown-skinned men with muscular builds, crowded around Jim—pale-faced, clean-shaven. He arranged our boxes of belongings to be carried, wiping the sweat from his brow. The scar on his forehead seemed more noticeable than ever. Watching, I thought, *Jim looks handsome in spite of his scar.* At six feet two inches, my thin lanky husband stood taller by half a foot than the Managalasi men. His brown crew-cut contrasted strongly with the mounds of dark woolly hair they wore high on their heads. Jim assigned each man a box of our belongings to carry over the trail to the empty house we would live in until construction on our house was completed.

A gray-haired man with a furrowed forehead approached Jim and waited for a box. The shredded, worn loincloth he wore did not quite cover him in the back. Jim handed him our Coleman pressure lamp. It wasn't too heavy, and bore a handle, which made it easy to carry.

"We've got a long walk ahead of us," Jim reminded me. "Why don't you get started and I'll catch up?" I looked around helplessly, not knowing where to start. "Just follow the boys who are carrying our boxes. They know where to go," he added, as though he had read my mind.

I was wearing my new Keds and plodded after the long stream of people heading up the mountain. Three young girls, about junior high age, hurried to my side to walk along with me.

The boys were eager to help carry our cargo.

The hill was long and steep. Thick, tall grass, shimmering in waves beneath the sun, grew on both sides of the dirt path. The heat staggered me, and about halfway up the hill each breath began to feel like fire in my chest. My parched throat cried out for a drink. The image of an ice-cold Coke, with frost forming on the glass, floated to mind. With no chance of drinking a Coke for six months, I fought to block the image from my thoughts.

After ten minutes, I was exhausted, and stood motionless, waiting for my second wind. The girls stopped, too, not seeming to mind that I was holding them up. One girl wore a huge smile and reached into the stringbag atop her head and drew out a piece of sugarcane. Then, with red teeth, she ripped off a section of the peeling. Soon she had the entire stalk peeled. She broke off a knot and handed it to me. Gratefully, I bit into it and sucked its juicy sweetness. Turning the sugarcane in my hands, I continued biting and sucking, not caring that the juice ran down my chin onto my dress. Slowly my thirst was being quenched, and I thanked the Lord for the simple gift of sugarcane which, in that moment of desperation, was worth more to me than gold.

Before we reached the top of the mountain, the skies began to change. Dark clouds blotted out the brilliant blue. At the top stood Koeno Village, one of forty Managalasi villages. The trail went towards the entrance of Koeno then curved off and immediately plunged into a descent, steeper than the hill we had just climbed.

As the girls and I were about midway down, rain sprinkled from the sky, then quickly came pelting down. One young man ahead of us slipped on the trail and the box he carried went flying. The girls exploded into laughter, snorting and snickering until they were faint of breath.

Soaked to the skin, I plowed on, straight downward, thankful for the rain that cooled my body and drove away the thirst. After a few minutes I found it difficult to stay on my feet. The mud beneath my not-so-new-anymore Keds felt slick as glass. I could hardly keep my balance. The girls, now in back of me, ceased chattering, and all was silent except for the squish of mud under our feet. Each time I skidded, they said a word that sounded like "whey," but no laughter followed. Then, without warning, my feet flew out from under me, and I was sitting on my bottom in the mud. Instantly the three girls were at my side with worried looks on their faces. "Ese, ese," they repeated as they helped me up. *Ese, the word they use for a greeting must also be used to say, "I'm sorry."*

"Thank you," I said in English and smiled. They smiled back. As we walked on down, the chubbiest of the three girls took my hand to protect me from falling again, but the pathway was too steep, too slippery. I fell harder the second time, pulling the young girl down with me. Within seconds she was back up on her feet, looking around to see if anyone witnessed her fall. But I sat there, covered with soupy mud, my hair clinging to my face in soaken strands and my clothes sticking to my body. *If only Mom could see me now,* I thought, and couldn't suppress the smile that came to my lips.

The other two, filled with concern, ran to us saying something in Managalasi. It was my turn to giggle now. At first the girls looked at each other, not sure how to respond. Then they joined me in laughter as they pulled me to my feet. Although we couldn't communicate a word to each other, a kinship passed between us, drawing us together, and I knew I had gained three friends.

At the bottom of the hill a small creek gurgled, but there was no way around it. We plunged in, and with each step, the oozing mud swallowed my Keds. After crossing the water, I paused to study the trail ahead. It went almost straight up. I sighed, trudged up the steep, slippery bank and followed a path beneath coconut trees. All of a sudden, I heard a lot of yelling ahead. The girls took off running, and I tried to keep up with them. Then I saw a man lying face down on the trail. As I got closer, I recognized the face of the man who had carried our pressure lamp. Beside him lay the lamp, now dented, with the glass broken into a thousand slivers. The older man's expression portrayed shock. He was not saying anything, nor making any attempt to get up. His left leg trembled uncontrollably. *Why wasn't somebody helping him?* I wondered.

I stared at the men standing nearby. They gawked at the dear old man and muttered to one another. Finally, one young man with very light skin began to shout: "Taupa! Taupa! Simamo... Taupa...Simamo!" He didn't seem to be shouting at anyone in particular.

"Taupa!" he yelled again and caught me staring wide-eyed at him. He smiled sheepishly, then turned to evade my stare.

Miraculously, Jim appeared from nowhere. He quickly knelt in the mud to pry the old man's fingers from the handle of the lamp.

"It's all right, it's all right," he said in English, helping the old man gently to his feet. Putting his hand under the frightened man's arm, he walked slowly along the path with him.

I looked around for my young companions, but they were nowhere in sight, so I traipsed along behind Jim and the old man.

Twenty minutes later, we reached the government rest house. It was a small house built to shelter government visitors in the days of the Australian administration. It consisted of a simple room constructed on stilts and it stood a few feet from the path. Plaited bamboo was tied onto poles to form walls. The thatched roof had gaping holes through which the rain now drizzled.

Sitting at the top of the ladder-like steps, I watched the men arrive with our boxes. Jim tried to pay them, but they only looked blankly at the coins in Jim's hand and walked away.

Why don't they want to get paid? I wondered as man after man refused the shillings Jim offered them. These indigenous people who lived without electricity, plumbing, televisions and washing machines must surely want something.

Hmm—plumbing! "Jim!" I yelled out. "What about a toilet?"

"Oh, I'll build one tomorrow. Just go in the bush for now."

The incredulous look on my face clearly summed up my feelings.

"No one will see," he added. "Just go far enough and look for a big tree."

Unhappily, I climbed down the steps and headed for the woods. But no matter how far I went, the sound of voices followed. I felt people could still see me, that they lurked behind trees watching. Better wait till dark, I concluded, walking quickly back to the clearing.

On the grass next to the burlap bag of salt stood our primus (a one-burner kerosene stove) reminding me that breakfast had been almost ten hours ago. *I'll get something cooking,* I told myself. *Then maybe I won't feel so depressed. But where's the kerosene? Which box held our cooking pots, food, matches, dishes? Oh boy, why didn't I think about labeling these boxes?* Realizing the hopelessness of finding anything now sent another wave of depression washing over me.

I noticed my three friends sitting along the path, joining others who sat in clumps on the grass.

Jim stood with a man who had just arrived from the airstrip with one of our boxes. Like all the others, this man shook his head, refusing the money in Jim's hand. But instead of leaving, he motioned to Jim with his thumb and middle finger, rubbing them together. "Misa," he said, looking hopefully at Jim, then repeated the word.

Those sitting on the grass looked up quickly and joined in. "Misa," they echoed. My three friends stood up immediately and looked over at me saying "misa." Big smiles lit their faces. All three rubbed their thumbs against their middle fingers, repeating the word. The chubbiest of the three sashayed over to me, pulled a potato from her stringbag, and rubbed two fingers over the top in a sprinkling-type motion. Then she pretended to take a bite. After imaginary swallowing, she looked heavenward and acted out eating food with zest. Her two buddies giggled from the sideline.

All at once I understood what the girl was trying to communicate—what everyone was trying to communicate.

"Jimmy!" I yelled excitedly. "These people don't want to get paid with money. They want salt! 'Misa' is their word for salt!"

"Oh, good, we have plenty of that," he said, moving towards the burlap bag. Jim reached for his penknife and slit open the top of the bag. The girls were right beside him and knew instantly what the bag contained. "Whee," they squealed.

In no time the men lined up, holding large leaves onto which Jim dispensed the salt. The men eyed each other with huge smirks that said it all.

Later, the carriers gradually drifted homeward under a darkening sky. As we unrolled our sleeping bags, an old woman approached us with two steaming potatoes—a gift. I wondered how she could hold such huge, hot potatoes without burning her fingers. "Thank you," we said in English. The woman smiled back. "Ese," she said, and hurried away. I looked at Jim. "Ese?" I repeated. "The word they use for 'hello' and 'I'm sorry,' also means good-bye?"

"Yes," Jim confirmed. "I learned that on my first visit."

Boy, did those potatoes hit the spot! Jim and I were hungry enough to have eaten them raw. Bone tired, we snuggled down into our sleeping bags. The night was clear, and we could see the moon overhead through the holes in the thatch.

"Why would the Managalasis want money anyway?" I remarked to Jim. "Where would they spend it? What could they buy with money out here?"

"Nothing," he replied in a voice that told me he was on the edge of sleep.

"Yet it doesn't seem fair to pay them a few tablespoons of salt for carrying heavy boxes up and down the mountain," I added. "But did you see how their eyes lit up when you spooned the salt onto the leaves?"

There was no response, and I knew Jim was asleep, but all I could do was lie there wide awake, looking up at the moon and myriads of stars. Reflecting on the day, I marvelled at how different our beds were from the night before—how different life was going to be.

Long before I met Jim, I knew God wanted me to be a missionary. Still, the words of Miss Lucinda swarmed through my brain like stinging hornets. "New Guinea? What a horrible place to live! And what about your children? Why will you deprive them of all America has to offer? You're selfish people! That's what I hate about missionaries!"

Reality was settling in hard. *Was this the place we would live for the rest of our lives? Would our children grow up—deprived?* Even though I knew I was where God wanted me, I could not help wondering. As Satan hurled his fiery darts of doubt, I tossed and turned on the bamboo floor, taking a "hit" with each dark thought.

I awoke to what sounded like hundreds of birds chirping, each singing a unique melody all its own. I wondered why God didn't create people like He did the birds—happy and without concern.

Jim was already up, sifting through cardboard boxes. "What are you looking for?" I asked.

"I thought you'd be wanting coffee, so I filled the primus with kerosene, found the sugar and coffee, but guess what—there's no water."

"Oh, that's right, there's no sink in this motel," I quipped. "How do we get water?"

"There's a bunch of kids outside. I'll see if one of them will fetch some."

Jim picked up both galvanized buckets and went outside. I peeked through a hole in the loosely woven bamboo wall and saw a group of young boys wearing loincloths that barely covered the necessary parts. As soon as they spotted Jim ambling towards them, they diffused in a dozen directions with the speed of light.

"Hey! Come back! We need water!" I heard Jim yell as I inched down deeper into my sleeping bag. The glorious sun beckoned me to get out of bed and unpack, but despondency, strong and bold, chained me down. The homesick feeling of wanting to return to New Jersey still engulfed me.

I've got to rise above this, I chided myself. *No true missionary should feel the way I do...choosing to forget about lost souls and go home. No Spirit-filled woman would have her every thought filled with loved ones left behind, or have this intolerable longing to be with them.*

I pushed my thoughts far back into the dark corner of my mind reserved for the inadmissable. *Yes! I must now think about my new life with the Managalasi people.* Before I could slip back into the forbidden, I unzipped the sleeping bag, shot up and dressed quickly. As I stepped outside the house, the sunlight perked up my spirits. Jim stood with three young men who looked like they could be teenagers. He held up a bucket with one hand and pointed towards the sound of rushing water with the other. The young men took the buckets and headed for the water.

"C'mon, let's unpack a few things," Jim said. He seemed relieved, now that water was on the way. We unpacked only the items we would need until we could move into our own house.

The boys returned and carried the water into the house. Beads of perspiration shimmered on their faces. Jim spooned salt onto three large leaves and handed one to each boy. "Thank you," we said. They responded with big smiles.

Feeling bold, I pointed to myself and said, "Judy." Then I pointed to my husband who was now pumping the primus. "Jim," I said. "Jim," they repeated together. Wanting them to say my name as well, I pointed to myself again and said, "Judy," but they just looked at each other. Then they laughed nervously, muttering into their cupped hands.

Bothered, I pointed to the tallest of the three. "Isoro," he said promptly, and then "Nuniha Isoro." Quickly, I picked up my pad and pencil and wrote down the name and then the phrase. He must be saying "My name is Isoro," I reasoned. Then I pointed to the other two and wrote "Chululu" and "Raka." Before they left I elicited the words for "water" and "bucket." Then I was ready for coffee.

For breakfast I dunked a "boi" biscuit into a steaming hot cup of instant Folgers, and Jim did the same with a cup of Milo, a chocolate drink made in Australia. "These biscuits are hard as nails. They're gonna break my teeth," Jim complained.

"I like them," I said, and crunched off a corner with my back teeth. "It's like eating giant saltine crackers."

After breakfast Jim suggested walking to the village to see what was going on. I grabbed my notebook and a pencil, and Jim reached for his machete—the one issued to us during field training in Mexico. The blade was at least three feet long; it looked treacherous. "What are you going to do with that?" I asked.

"Oh, I thought if the men were clearing the land for our house, I'd help," he replied.

Jim stabbed at the ground with the knife as we walked to Numba Village. The entrance was flanked by long rows of brilliant poinsettias. Dewdrops glistened on red bracts with yellow centers. "Wow!" I said, surprised. "I never expected to see poinsettias growing here. Aren't they beautiful? Just like a picture out of *National Geographic*."

"Yeah," Jim grunted. "And they grow all year round, not just at Christmas time like in New Jersey."

I sniffed the air. The fragrance of fresh jungle greenery mixed with smoke from a wood fire filled my nostrils as we entered the village. When the young boys and girls saw us, they scrambled off into the bushes behind houses. Just before they disappeared, they glanced back to make sure we weren't following. A woman

Plaiting bamboo to replace an inside wall,
this Numba man barely acknowledged our presence.

sitting on the ground got up quickly, scooped up her baby and scurried into the house. Some older men remained sitting on the ground, plaiting large pieces of flattened bamboo. They kept their eyes down, as if afraid to look at us. I fought off the dreadful feeling of being unwanted.

"Ese!" we called out. All three looked up quickly and responded with "Esa'ua."

"Esa'ua," we repeated, and I quickly wrote down the word. "That's a little different type of greeting," Jim remarked to me. "I wonder what the difference is."

"I suppose we'll find out. Let's try to get their names."

"Nuniha Judy," I said slowly. The men looked at each other without glancing up and muttered something.

"Ese, sistah," they said finally.

"No, no! Not sistah," I insisted, recognizing the Australian term for "nurse." How could I convey to them I wasn't a nurse?

Again I pointed at myself. "Judy," I enunciated. The three men looked at each other with embarrassed expressions.

"Nuniha Jim," my husband said, and their response was immediate. "Jim, ese," they said and I grew frustrated. Why will they only acknowledge Jim and not me?

"Did you notice they said 'ese' this time?" Jim asked. "It must be used for greeting one person."

"Esa'ua," he said back to the men. This time they all smiled and nodded. "Ese, Jim." That they accepted Jim readily but not me was irritating. I looked around and spotted Chululu and Isoro lounging on the ground in front of one of the houses. "I'm going over to talk to the boys," I said to Jim and strolled in their direction.

The village was as round as a cake. The houses built on stilts stuck up like candles on the cake. Pandanus leaves crowned each rectangular shaped home. I was amazed by the attractive designs neatly woven into the bamboo walls. But it was all so colorless. Everything was a dismal brown from the rooftops to the bare ground. *Someone needs to plant red poinsettias inside the village, too—a lot of them,* I thought.

Isoro and Chululu talked with an old woman who sat near the doorway of her house smoking a long, bamboo pipe. Designs like the ones hand-painted onto their bark skirts were etched into the bamboo walls.

"Esa'ua!" I called out, proud that I could greet them using the correct plural form. The older woman looked up from her pipe and nodded. "Ese!" the boys said. "Sistah, ese!"

"No! No!" I said, shaking my head wildly at the boys. "Ju-dee," I said loudly, and wondered why on earth they wouldn't say my name. I pressed further, "Nuniha Ju-dee. JU-DEE. JEW-DEEE!" At my outburst, the two of them exploded into laughter. The old woman pointed her pipe at the boys and spoke sharply, bringing their laughter to an abrupt halt. They stiffened visibly beneath the old woman's glare, and she continued to scold them.

What's going on? my scrambled mind puzzled. *Why will these people say Jim's name but not mine? Could it be that in this culture they didn't call a woman by her first name, or was there something wrong?*

From a slight distance, I stood watching the gray-haired woman. Her eyes, like fire, burned into both boys. She waved her bamboo pipe menacingly at them, bombarding them with harsh words. They sat sheepishly with eyes downcast, looking as though they would like to disappear.

"What's she angry about?" asked a voice behind me. It was Jim.

"I wish I knew," I said. "I was just trying to get the boys to say my name, and they laughed. I imagine she's scolding them for laughing, but I'm not sure."

"Too bad we didn't bring the tape recorder. I'd love to know what she's saying," Jim said, then tugged on my arm. "Let's go to the other village."

"What other village?"

"Sivurani Village. Numba is only one of many Managalasi villages, you know. Our house'll be built midway between this one and Sivurani. C'mon, I'll take you there now."

"Let's go," I said, relieved to hear we would not have to live in Numba. Something about this village fogged my mind with subtle despair.

A narrow pathway led away from Numba Village down a hill between beautiful jungle foliage. Neatly trimmed grass bordered each side of the path. At the bottom of the incline we saw a clearing in the brush. "Our house will be built right there," Jim said. "That's the piece of land Lotuli gave us." We didn't know then that it was the scar on Jim's forehead that induced Lotuli to give us this land to build our house.

In the beginning, when Jim came with an interpreter to get permission to live with the Managalasis, they did not want us. "The last time Americans were here, there was a war," they informed Jim through the interpreter. "We don't want any more Americans to come." All the Numba Village men agreed—except Lotuli.

Lotuli was a V.I.P. from Numba Village. During droughts the people depended on him to make the rains come. And Lotuli could do it. The rainmaker communicated with spirits, and, using their power, he could make the rains stop as well as bring them on.

After seeing Jim for the first time, Lotuli had a dream. "Jim is your brother," a voice told him in the dream.

Lotuli's older brother died during tribal warfare many years before when an enemy sliced open his forehead with an axe and killed him.

"Jim is your older brother who has returned from the dead as a white man," the voice revealed. "Look at Jim's forehead and you will see the mark where he was struck and killed."

Seeing the scar on Jim's forehead convinced Lotuli.

So, while the Numba men told Jim "No," Lotuli offered the white man a piece of his land to build a house. He was, after all, obliged to take care of his family, the oldest brother being the most important family member.

The rainmaker's gift of land angered the Numba people, and from the cool reception we just received in the village, I knew they were still angry.

As we approached Lotuli's land, Jim asked, "What do you think?"

"Looks like a perfect spot. It'll be like having our own private nook between the villages."

"It will work out perfectly," Jim said, and squatted by a stack of poles tied with jungle vines. He ran his hand along the pole on top. "If we had to choose one village to live in, it might isolate us from the other one. But by living on this piece of land, we can belong to both villages and have a little privacy at the same time...that is, if we ever get our house built; these poles aren't going to be big enough," he said, looking disappointed. "And we'll have termites gnawing at them in no time. There's got to be better wood than this. Oh, well," he said and shrugged acceptingly. "Let's go to Sivurani."

We walked beside a row of betelnut trees that arched gracefully over the pathway leading up to Sivurani Village. As soon as we arrived, several villagers ran to us yelling, "Esa'ua!" One young girl put her hand in mine and started leading me around the village. I felt welcome, and that was a good feeling. Jim stayed behind with a group of men sitting on mats outside chewing betelnut. *How different it seems from the first village,* I thought, warmed by the enthusiastic greeting. Then I saw grass and flowers planted around the houses. They made a world of difference.

"Jim!" I called, and looked back to see him showing his machete to the men. A few more had gathered around him. Jim looked over at me. "Can we plant some of these beautiful red flowers around our house?" I asked.

"Sure, why not? We can probably plant whatever you want."

The young girl pulled me along gently, turning around to smile at me every once in a while. This village was at least twice the size of Numba, long and oval-shaped rather than round. The sun felt delightfully warm on my shoulders as we meandered past thatched houses on stilts built close to the edge of the mountain ridge. The bare earth in the center of the village was tidy, as if it had been freshly swept.

Warm, laughing people welcomed me to Sivurani Village.

Squawk! A perky mynah bird sat on an exposed rafter on a rooftop, and scolded young boys playing beside the house.

"Ese!" a familiar voice called out. Surprised, I turned to see one of the three girls who had walked with me from the airstrip. It was the chubby one who liked to laugh. She sat in the doorway, legs folded beneath her, and a big smile beamed a welcome to me. Her sturdy body hinted at femininity and, like the other women in the village, she wore a piece of bark cloth like a wraparound skirt with bright red and yellow designs painted on it. A vine, worn as a knotted belt, fastened the cloth just below her thick waist.

When I reached her house, she broke off part of the ash-encrusted yam she was eating and handed it to me. "Oh, oh," I thought, "should I eat this or not? Lord, you know I can't insult my new friend by refusing this yam, but is it clean? Will I get sick? Please protect me!" My prayer was like an S.O.S., but I felt a lot better about eating the yam after sending up the request.

"Ese," my friend said again and moved over, making room for me to sit beside her.

Reaching in my pocket, I pulled out my pen and notebook. "My name is Judy," I said in the best Managalasi I knew. Then I pointed to her. "Sonalu," she said with laughter in her eyes, and I wrote it down. Then I began pointing to the things inside the house. Sonalu got the idea quickly and began telling me words faster than I could write. I tried to repeat each word until I could say it to her satisfaction. Some of the words were long and difficult to repeat. Sonalu hooted with laughter whenever I made a mistake. *Oh man,* I thought, *I'll never learn to speak this language*. But Sonalu didn't seem to mind repeating the words till I got them right.

I heard the men talking and looked over to see they were still examining Jim's machete. An older bare-breasted woman, wanting to see what interested the men, approached them boldly. Her confidence disappeared when she saw the machete. "Whey!" she said, and backed up a few short steps. Then she ran back to her house and disappeared inside. The men laughed uproariously.

I turned to face Sonalu. Her dark eyes smiled at me over the top of the yam she held to her mouth. Her warmth reached out to me, and I smiled back at her. It was impossible not to.

There was easiness in Sivurani Village; warmth, laughter, color. The tension and gloom I felt in Numba seemed non-existent here. I could work with these people. Everything was going to be all right.

No one asked about my name during our first visit to Sivurani. But, as Jim and the men were building our house, many young people approached me and, with smirks on their faces, asked, "What's your name?"

"Ju-dee," I would say, enunciating both syllables. Without fail, the young people laughed openly, then went off snickering. When older people were in hearing distance, they used a string of scorching words, and sent the offenders scurrying on their way.

After one week, the frame of the house was standing, the thatch roof tied on, and the woven bamboo walls fastened to the frame with nails we had brought from Ukarumpa. Jim cut large window holes in the walls, providing us with a fantastic view of the jungle from every room.

My favorite feature of the house was the half-wall around the porch. Jim had sawed a pile of bamboo tubes into four-foot lengths, stood them upright and tied them together with vine. A long piece of bamboo lay across the half-wall, acting as a railing. The half-wall added charm to our brown, drab house. Lastly, the young people planted the red flowers I admired so much all around the house. They chatted happily as they planted together and seemed excited that we chose those particular flowers. Two weeks after our arrival, we moved in.

One morning, several weeks later, I stood at the kitchen "counter"—a thick board taken from one side of our packing crate—fixing Jim a cup of Milo. I looked up and recognized an old woman bent forward beneath the load of her stringbag, as she walked by the house.

"Avami, where are you going?" I yelled to her with the confidence of having mastered the phrase. She stopped abruptly and turned to squint at me from under the burden on her head. "I'm going to the garden," she said. The wide smile on her face told me she was glad I spoke in her language.

Avami, my village mother, could carry more weight on her head than her body weight.

"Wait!" I called, and, grabbing my pen and pad, ran out to the path where Avami stood waiting. "Sit down," I said and reached to help remove the stringbag.

"No! No!" she scolded and sat down with the bag still suspended from her head. Then she leaned back and the stringbag fell off easily. Flopping down next to her, I put the strap of the bag on my head and tried to get up. The weight of the bag held me down, and I could not move.

The old woman looked at me and laughed. "Wait!" she said, getting up. By now a group of young boys had gathered to watch.

Avami took the weight of the bag in her arms, allowing me to stand. After I was up, she let go and I felt the bag pull on the muscles in my neck. Imitating a Managalasi woman, I bent forward. But when I tried to walk, I couldn't keep my balance and wobbled like someone who had too much to drink. The young boys hooted.

Avami helped me sit down again and, after taking off the stringbag, spoke to the boys in a controlled tone. A look of horror crossed their faces and they plugged their ears with their fingers. I knew she was reprimanding them for laughing at me, but what words did she use to put such fear into them? Then, all of a sudden, she put a gnarled forefinger between her teeth and, like a witch, started towards them with a wild look. The boys howled and ran as if a horde of demons raced in pursuit. When they were out of sight, Avami came back. Suddenly a coughing spasm overtook her.

"Sit down and I'll bring you something to drink," I said and ran to the kitchen. Jim came out carrying the handscale. I ran past him without a word. Hastily, I spooned two scoops of Milo into a cup, poured the hot water, stirred vigorously and flew out again. Jim stood next to Avami and, using both hands, held up the scale with her stringbag suspended from it.

"Guess what this weighs," Jim said, his breath nearly gone.

"Fifty pounds," I wagered. I handed the Milo to Avami.

"Not even close—it weighs 103 pounds!"

"What? It can't be! Avami can't weigh more than ninety pounds herself," I said, astonished. Then I felt embarrassed, since I couldn't even walk a few steps with the bag, and especially so because I far outweighed my skinny-as-a-bamboo-pole friend. "How can these little old ladies carry such heavy loads?"

"Well, just think about it," Jim said, "the girls start carrying a stringbag on their heads as soon as they can walk. They train for it while growing up, I guess, and just get used to it."

As Jim headed toward the house, I turned back to Avami. The wild, almost animal look had disappeared from her face, and she sipped the chocolate drink appearing satisfied. I decided that now was a good time to ask about my name. In poor Managalasi I asked: "Why people call Jim's name, but not call my name?"

She understood what I meant and replied immediately. "Your name is no good!" She practically spit the words at me.

My mouth dropped open. "What?"

"It's no good!" she snarled, disdain all over her face. She placed a betelnut between blackened teeth and cracked down on the outer shell. She carefully removed the precious nut from the green shell and fumbled in the stringbag with her left hand. "I'm going to give you a new name," she announced before popping the nut into her mouth. She pulled two pepper leaves from her stringbag and chewed them with the nut.

Speechless, I sat and watched my new friend reach for a pear-shaped gourd, remove the woven lid, and dig inside with a cassowary bone. I hoped she would say more about my name, and tell me why it was no good.

Avami scraped some white lime powder from her gourd, then licked the bone clean. "I'm going to name you 'Dzaki,'" she declared through a mouthful of leaves, nut and lime. She rolled the three ingredients in her mouth until the consistency resembled a huge wad of chewing tobacco that turned as red as blood. She looked at me with a twinkle in her eye and a smile that plainly revealed the mixture. A bit of the juice trickled down one corner of her mouth which she wiped quickly with the back of her hand.

"Here, Dzaki," she said, handing me a nut and some pepper leaves. Then her eyes challenged mine. "You chew some too!"

Oh, no, I don't want to eat that awful stuff, I thought. I looked at her eager face watching mine, longing for me to share her "brew."

Slowly, I cracked the green outer shell with my teeth just like she did. So far so good, I thought. Next I picked out the white nut nestled inside and put it to my mouth. One slight touch to my tongue and the puckering sensation sent chills through my whole body. I felt my mouth shriveling up, and my tongue strangely thick.

In double-quick time, I stood to my feet and covered my mouth with my hand. Avami sat laughing softly, as if she knew this would happen. "Avami, sorry," I started to say, but there was no saliva in my mouth, and my lips were too parched to speak. I dropped the remaining nut and leaves onto her lap and took off for the house. *Water...I have to have water!*

"Good-bye, my daughter, I'm going to the garden now," I heard Avami call out as I drank greedily from the cool, boiled water in our drinking container. Daughter? She called me her daughter. Elated, I rushed out to the porch to say good-bye, but the old woman was already on her way down the trail. "Good-bye, Mother!" I yelled through lips that still smarted.

I went back inside to tell Jim the news about my name. He sat at his desk conjugating verbs with Isai, his language helper.

"Guess what!" I said, bursting in on their session. "Avami said my name is no good. I wonder what it means."

Right away Jim turned to Isai. "What does 'Judy' mean?" he asked in Managalasi.

"It's a bad word in our language," Isai affirmed, smiling nervously. Isai was timid, and rarely looked at Jim when speaking to him. "When women are present, men don't say that word."

"Oh, brother," I said in English to Jim. "Why, of all places in the world, would God send us to a village where my name has a bad connotation?"

Jim's mouth twitched to keep from grinning. "I suppose we'll find out one day, but it may not be till we get to heaven."

"Well, I'm 'Dzaki' now," I informed him and watched his eyebrows rise in surprise.

"Where'd you get that name?"

"From my Managalasi 'mother,'" I answered, holding my head high. Then I left the pair of them to study their verbs.

"Dzaki," I repeated to myself as I pumped the primus to reheat the water for coffee. "Lord," I prayed, "I don't understand why You led us to a language area where my name has a bad meaning, but I won't mind being called Dzaki (Jaki) at all."

Months crept by. There seemed to be nothing new to add to my dictionary file, and language learning idled to a standstill. Relating to the women was difficult because I could not do the simple tasks they performed every day, like carrying a stringbag on my head, roasting a yam, or getting a fire going without dozens of matches and candles.

"Jim will surely take another wife," I overheard one of the women say. "The wife he's got doesn't know how to work in the garden or make a fire with sticks. All she does is make marks on paper everyday. She's useless."

Since two village men had taken two wives each, bigamy was not a new concept. "I wonder who Jim will take," the women whispered.

Our supplies were getting lower and lower. At night I would dream about sinking my teeth into fresh, warm, melt-in-your-mouth fudge. Then, when our sugar ran out, despair swallowed me, consuming my joy and courage.

In the morning, I'd force myself out of bed, cross another day off the calendar, crawl back in and lie there most of the day. Painful longing to see Mom carved a hollow in my breast, and despondency seemed to fill it. I desperately needed to be with my own kind of people. I couldn't bring myself to go to the villages and visit any, so I remained in the house, alienating myself from the people in our village.

Jim worked contentedly with Isai every day, and that irritated me. My husband was actually enjoying himself. He grew up on a farm in the mountains of Tennessee and felt right at home living in an isolated setting. However, I grew tired of being in the same place for weeks on end and missed the city life. From my hometown in New Jersey, I could see New York's skyline. Now I could vividly see those bright lights in my mind, and they called out to me more than ever.

I whined to Jim, "If I could just hop into the car once in a while and drive to a diner for pie and coffee, I'd be happy."

"That's impossible, so forget about it!" he said, unmoved. "You can't stay in the house all day like this; the people can feel your desertion. You've got to get out there and visit with them!"

Can't Jim see what's wrong? I wondered. *Are all men insensitive to the things women feel? Well, even if Jim doesn't understand how I feel, God does. If I gave up and went home, He would understand. God loves me deeply, no matter what.* But I knew there would be another matter to contend with. Thoughts of my pastor's blue eyes smoldering from behind the pulpit swirled to mind.

Dr. Charles Anderson, the pastor of Brookdale Baptist Church in Bloomfield, New Jersey, had preached, "Keep your commitments to God or die trying!" The truth of those words nagged at me. If I gave up and went home, I'd have no excuse to give my pastor.

After much pondering, I discovered that my real battle was, *Do I love God enough to tough it out? Can I live with people who are not "my kind" so that they can share eternity in heaven?*

As I labored with this emotional and spiritual question, laughter, like waves of light breaking into darkness, drifted from Sivurani Village into my kitchen. "Who's that?" I called to Jim and Isai in the study.

"It's Sonalu," Isai called back.

I got up and went to speak to Isai. "Would Sonalu help me learn the language every day like you help Jim?" I asked.

Isai acted shy whenever we asked about single girls. Now he laughed uneasily. "I don't know."

"And I need someone to help with laundry, too," I added.

"Sonalu is coming now," Isai said, looking uncomfortable. "Ask her."

By the time I reached the porch, Sonalu was almost to the front steps. After greeting her, I got right to the point. "Sonalu, can you work for me every day?"

She looked at me quizzically. "I don't understand," she said.

"Jimmy-o!" I called loudly. "Tell Isai to come and explain to Sonalu about working for me."

In a few minutes, they both appeared. Isai hesitated in his usual shy manner. Then I remembered their culture prohibited unrelated boys and girls from speaking directly to one another.

I watched Isai, with his eyes averted, explaining shyly to Sonalu what I had said. As he talked, Sonalu's eyes brightened, and the puzzled look changed to one of pleasure. She looked at me and her smile beamed consent. *Happy day! Now I'll have a companion to show me how to roast yams, to help me speak the language better; I'll have a reason to get up in the morning. I'll teach her how to drink coffee, and we'll be friends.*

In no time, the two of us were heading down the mountain toward the river. Sonalu carried the laundry in a bucket on her head and I took my pencil and pad. Once again I felt ready to get down to the business of learning this language.

"Listen to the many birds singing," I said in simple Managalasi. "Don't they sound beautiful?"

"No," Sonalu answered abruptly. "It makes me mad to hear them."

"Why?" I asked, surprised.

"Because I can't eat them, that's why!" she said, rubbing her meat-hungry stomach. My new helper caught the look of surprise on my face and erupted into boisterous laughter. Her guffawing continued on and on. It was contagious, and I laughed with her. Laughing together was like a tonic. As I felt the depression lifting away, I knew Sonalu was God's gift to me.

Later that night as I lay in bed, my mind too active to let me sleep, I became deeply aware that friends and churches around the world were praying for me. They must have been praying all along. I wanted to thank God for them and for His provisions.

Dear Heavenly Father, I do not understand why You chose me, nor why You even allow me to keep living when my faith is so small. Thank You for Your mercy, Your patience, and for Your love.

Thank You especially for all those who pray for us, for the prayers of the people at our home church in Bloomfield, for Mom, for friends and churches around the world.

Thank You for Dr. Anderson whose unwavering preaching has helped mold my thinking according to Your Word.

Thank You, Lord, for giving me Sonalu, who has a happy, laughing personality like Mom's to help me through lonely times.

Thank You, Father, for keeping me from giving up, for giving me the desire to tough it out, because these Managalasi people for whom You died are worth it.

The villagers called him "Olempoka," but Jim shortened the name to "Poki." The nickname caught on and soon all the villagers were calling him Poki. He said he was born three gardens after Mt. Lamington erupted which would make him eight years old now. Birth records were not kept, and the volcano's eruption helped us gauge how old the people were, discounting the very old ones.

Poki could mimic everyone in the village. It didn't take long for his audience, mostly young boys, to identify who he was mimicking and collapse with unrestrained laughter. Neither Jim nor I understood all that he said, yet we couldn't help but laugh at his antics. It was clear the boys idolized him.

Instead of helping his father with garden work, the young imitator chose to sit around our house all day and wait for Jim to finish his work with Isai. Like a puppy, he was constantly at Jim's side—telling him legends, ready to start a fire for him, fetch water, or do whatever needed to be done. In the afternoon,

Jim would get his shotgun and the two of them would go off into the woods and hunt for wallabies, tree kangaroos or birds.

"Jim never misses," Poki would brag to the village people, dangling fresh meat in front of their awestruck faces.

The pair of them would bring back enough game for every family to cook with their yams. Anyone who could provide meat was a hero, and Jim was held in high esteem.

"Jim builds good houses, and he's a good hunter," the village people would say, "but Jaki...all she does is stay at home and make marks on paper. What good is that?"

One morning Poki agreed to guide us over the mountain to visit Isai in his garden. As soon as we left the village site, we were in dense jungle, the trail barely visible. Vines hung from trees, some as thick as ropes. Parrots screamed at us from gnarled branches that dripped with moisture.

While we walked down the mountainside, Poki talked constantly. I caught a word here and there but not enough to understand what he was saying. A swirling brook gushed over rocks at the bottom of the mountain. As Jim reached out his hand to help me cross, he remarked, "When I can understand what Poki is saying, I'll know the language fluently."

"Soon," I encouraged, "you'll understand everything he says." As we started up the next mountain, I grew breathless and had to stop. I thought about the women who carried 100 pounds on their heads up and down these steep trails and marvelled at the prospect.

"I don't know how they do it," I remarked to Jim who stood patiently nearby.

"Huh? Who? What are you talking about?"

"I don't know how these slender women carry their produce, firewood, and sometimes even their babies up and down these mountains and never huff or puff."

"Because," he replied, "these 'slender' women are strong women in many ways."

The scent of wood burning in the distance reached my nostrils. Not sure how to use the possessive forms, I asked Poki in painful Managalasi, "Who fire that?"

"That's Avami's fire," he replied, pointing to the left. "Her garden is close by." I turned and saw the smoke rising a short distance from where we stood.

"Jim, let's drop by and see what she's doing."

Jim looked at Poki and motioned with his chin towards the smoke. "Let's go over there," he said.

Poki led us carefully across the garden, making sure we did not step on animal traps or newly planted yams. Limbs from trees were placed neatly around each crop, separating one from the other. The layout reminded me of a patchwork quilt. My favorite red-leafed plant grew everywhere, adding significant color to the browns and greens throughout the gardens.

Within minutes we approached the clearing where Avami and her husband, Inao, had built a lean-to shelter. I found my village mother cooking yams in the milk can I had given her.

"Ese, my daughter," she greeted with a radiant smile. "Where are you going?"

"We're going to Isai's garden," I said and sat down across from her.

"Stay and eat yams with us," she coaxed, ripping a large banana leaf into five pieces to use for plates. Inao, who was very light on his feet, came bounding over from the garden like a butterfly. “Ese!” he said over and over with a big smile. I knew they were genuinely glad we had come. So was I.

As we ate the yams mixed with leaves from a pumpkin vine, we talked in short sentences. Poki repeated everything we said to make sure the older couple understood. I felt excited—we were actually carrying on a conversation! All of a sudden, Avami thrust her hand in the air, hushing us to silence. The alert look on her face told us to listen. Then we all heard what she had heard.

Avami motioned to her husband and Poki. The three of them stood quietly and stalked towards the scratching sound. I had heard this sound many times in Sonalu’s house—a rat! But why were they making such a big deal about it?

Jim and I stood so we could see what was going on. Finally, they spotted their victim, and the three of them, with arms outstretched, moved in on it. Then quicker than lightning, Avami snagged the rat with a bony hand and, clamping her fingers around the throat, squeezed until the legs stopped kicking. I thought my eyes would pop from their sockets.

My “slender” mother picked up a knife and whacked off a piece of overhanging vine. With it she tied her prize to the lean-to, a triumphant smile on her face. Dinner would taste ever so much better that evening flavored with meat.

Poki, Jim, and I said our good-byes and started on the trail once more to Isai’s garden. Thinking about the rat, I asked: “Jim, would you have eaten that yam if you knew it was cooked with rat?”

“Sure, why not? The rats that run around in these gardens eat healthy foods, like potatoes, leaves and nuts. They don’t eat garbage, like rats at home.”

“Does that mean they’re safe to eat? No germs?”

"Yes, they're safe. It'd be no different than eating a pig, possum or any other animal."

We hiked in silence for a while. Then I called up ahead to Poki, "Why do Avami and Inao grow so many red flowers in their gardens? Do they eat those too?"

"No! No!" Poki said, and his tone grew serious. "Everybody plants red flowers in their gardens. They keep the bad spirits away. Some plant them around their houses too, like you did."

At that, Jim and I stopped dead in our tracks. Poki continued, "This way, when you're sleeping at night, the spirits won't come in and attack you."

Jim and I looked at each other for a long moment. "As soon as we get home," Jim said, "those plants have to be pulled up."

"Wait a minute," I countered. "Did you see how happy the people were who planted them for us? Maybe you'll offend them."

"That's okay! We'll find something else to plant around the house. Something that has nothing to do with spirits."

The idea of Jim and me messing with "spirit worship stuff" catapulted me up the mountainside. I earnestly hoped the Managalasis realized we didn't plant those leaves to appease any spirits.

Before long we reached Isai's garden. It was freshly burnt off and most of the yams already planted. Isai must have heard us coming. "Jim, I'm over here."

We found him building a table in the middle of the garden. As we approached, Isai was tying on the last leg—a bamboo pole—to the table top, constructed from several bamboos that were the length and diameter of a flute.

"Esa'ua, you've come," he said. He tried to smile, but his lips quivered.

Together we watched Isai put bits of yam, sweet potato, a few nuts, and finally a tiny dead animal onto the table.

"What are you doing?" Jim asked.

"I made this table for my mother," he said.

Putting food on the table for the spirits.

My eyes locked with Jim's in amazement. "But your mother is dead!" I blurted out, totally perplexed.

"That's true," he admitted and smiled nervously. "But her spirit is here, and if she gets hungry, she will come and eat the food."

Something bristled at the back of my neck. I wanted to tell Jim's tutor that it was useless to put food out for a dead person, and that his mother's spirit would not come and eat the food.

Jim tried his best to explain what happens after a person dies. But even Poki, who understood Jim better than any Managalasi person, could not make sense of what Jim tried to say.

We sat around on the bare ground chatting for a while. "I cooked yams. Are you hungry?" Isai offered.

"My stomach is full," I said. It was the Managalasi way to say you did not want to eat. "We ate yams with Avami and Inao."

After a few awkward moments, Isai stood and walked over by the table he had made. Then he gazed upward and yelled as loudly as he could: "Wato!"

Immediately, we recognized the word for "mother" and knew he was talking to her spirit. Jim flicked on the tape recorder he had carried from home. Isai did not see the recorder and continued his monologue unhampered.

Much later, after we had returned home, Poki helped us translate what had been recorded on the tape. Isai's talk to his mother was a prayer.

"Mother, come," he'd prayed. "See the table I built for you. See the special food I brought for you. Come and eat! Eat and be happy with my sacrifice. Be pleased and bless my garden. Give me a lot of food so I won't be hungry."

The reality of living in a world where Satan was god settled on us in full measure, and we began to realize the immensity of the task facing us. Isai's prayer sent cold chills down to my fingertips. He prayed to an ancestor spirit the same way we pray to God.

"How will we ever convince the Managalasis they're believing a lie?" I asked Jim over breakfast the next morning.

"It's not going to happen overnight, that's for sure," Jim replied. "Fortunately we don't have to worry about it; if God really wants us to tell these people about Him, the Holy Spirit will do the work, not us."

Even though I believed what Jim said, it seemed impossible to my finite mind that a people so steeped in animism could believe the Gospel; and the burden of these people's salvation lay heavily on me, as though it would be my fault if they didn't believe.

I cleaned up the breakfast dishes and then grabbed my novel. Sunday was like any other day to the village people and they were in their gardens planting. Looking forward to relaxing with the book I had been anxious to read, I headed out the front door and settle under a banana tree.

"Greetings!" a voice broke in behind me. It was Sonalu's older brother, Raka. His smile spread the width of his face.

"What are you doing?" he asked, joining me under the tree.

"Uh-oh," I thought. "How do I express 'reading' in the Managalasi language?"

"I'm counting words," I replied, choosing the closest idiom I could come up with.

"What words?" he asked, taking the book from my hands. "Where are they?" His eyes moved curiously from me to the book, then back to me again.

"It's uh, the words we uh, say with our mouths," I stuttered lamely and knew the words I wanted to say weren't coming out right. Feeling frustrated, I watched him staring hard at the book, trying to see words.

"There," I said, pointing to the fine print. "I look at these marks and I can hear my language."

Raka squinted at the strange marks, trying to make sense of them, then held the book up toward the sun to get a better look.

Finally he put the book next to his ear and waited, as if the words would speak to him if he waited long enough.

That's when it hit me—Raka didn't know what a book was. Probably no one else in the village knew, either.

The confused boy handed the book back to me and went on his way. As I watched his brown back disappear between the rows of banana trees, I knew I had to make a book with Managalasi words. These people needed to know what books were so they could have the joy of reading too. But how? I could barely speak the language, let alone get a book printed.

Dismissing my inadequacies, I went into the study and picked up the word file from my desk. It contained all the Managalasi words I was collecting for a dictionary.

Doggedly I went through each index card, making lists of short words. Next I started choosing words that had the same kinds of syllables. Hours passed as I agonized over how to make a primer. Finally I came up with a story about "father." It read:

"This is Father.

Father can see.

Father sees pigs.

Father sees coconuts.

Father sees yams."

Hooray! The first Managalasi book was underway! Excitement mounted until I thought I would burst. Then the flame in the kerosene lamp started flickering. Jim had gone to bed long ago, and I rushed to get ready for bed before the flame flickered out.

Dropping onto the thin mattress, I pulled the sheet around me and tried to sleep, but Raka's face kept looming before me. First it was eager and happy, then quizzical, and finally blank. It bothered me that Raka had never experienced the pleasure of reading. Well, he won't be kept waiting much longer, I promised myself. The time to teach is now, and that includes everybody in the village. Sleep finally came.

As the next morning dawned, I jumped out of bed with a new zest for life. My zeal pushed me into finishing the inspiring story about "Father." With a burning haste I illustrated each page. "Father" became a stick figure wearing a g-string. All the pigs had noses no real pig could ever have, but the squiggly tails at the other end made it clear they were pigs.

After laboriously making six copies by hand, I felt ready to round up the book-starved men. Off I went to Sivurani. I stood at the bottom end of the village and yelled out as loudly as I could: "All the men, come! Come and hear my talk!"

A few faces peered out from the doorways. Several children ran screaming into their houses. No one rushed out to meet me. Exercising patience, I leaned against a coconut tree and waited. A few young girls with stupid grins on their faces sauntered over and sat down. They looked at me and giggled. I turned in the other direction, completely ignoring them. It was the men I was after—the important, prestigious men. Learning to read and write must be made a special privilege to the community. Teaching silly girls would turn that privilege into something frivolous and unimportant. The men must learn first.

When most of the men finally gathered, I bravely held up the books and tried to convey how wonderful it was to "count words." Were they understanding my chopped-up Managalasi? I felt like a stammering two-year-old. Plunging on, I noticed most of the men looking away, as if embarrassed by what I was saying. When at last I finished, a heavy silence hung over us like a thick cloud.

In a voice I hoped sounded light and carefree I asked, "Who wants to learn to count words?" The entire group evaded my question, as if I had offended them. I singled out Binny. He had the most gardens and the community respected him.

"Binny," I called, and he cringed, "will you come to school tomorrow?"

He sat fidgeting with his hands for a while, then, "Our heads are too hard," he replied. "We can't learn. Teach the children; their heads are soft."

"If you come every morning without being lazy, you will learn," I insisted, fighting off the rejection.

Another spoke up: "We have to work in our gardens. Will learning to read help our gardens grow?"

Unprepared for this question I was taken aback, not sure how to answer. "You, uh, have to learn so you can, uh, read God's Book and, uh...." I stopped, for I could tell by the feel of them it was no use. Not one of them cared about God—yet.

Then, one of the giggly girls spoke up. "You have lots of dresses. Will you give us one if we come?" She eyed the dress I was wearing as she continued pleading. "We can't wear old, bark cloths inside your nice house."

"No, I will not," I snapped. I knew I shouldn't be talking this way, but I couldn't help it. I pressed on: "Learning is a good thing...," my voice trailed off into silence.

Part of the group was leaving, taking the last of my enthusiasm with them. Suppressing an urge to fling the readers to the wind, I turned and headed home.

That night as I lay on the bed, a feeling of defeat, compounded with awesome responsibility, swept over me. I began accusing God. "Lord, why did you send us here? You knew these people wouldn't be interested in reading."

It was all God's fault, and now I really want to go home. Ahh...home. The thought filled me with longing. *At home I could relax on a soft couch, speak my own language and be blissfully unaware of failure.*

The cheerful sun greeted me the next morning. Still it seemed useless to get up. I looked out the window and saw Sonalu hanging out clothes. A thought leaped to mind.

"Sonalu," I called, getting her attention. She was wearing a large navy and white handkerchief on her head and turned toward me looking for all the world like Aunt Jemima. "You're going to learn to count words," I yelled. "Come!"

I turned my back on her look of surprise, dressed and went outside to set up two kerosene drums. "Sit down," I said, patting the drum next to mine. Not wasting a moment, I opened the primer and began instructing. "This is 'ma,'" I said, pointing to the syllable. "Now you say it."

"Ma!" she yelled back so loudly, I dropped the book. She saw me jump and let out a hoot of laughter. "Sorry," she mumbled, still laughing. She covered her mouth to keep the laughter inside, but it only got worse. In awe, I gaped at her as she snickered and snorted. It became impossible not to laugh with her, and soon both of us were wiping tears from our eyes.

Settling down, we resumed class and Sonalu learned to read two pages. I was ecstatic! My primer was working! Long after class, Sonalu sat reading the same two pages over and over. Finally, my prodigy went home clutching the book proudly in her hand.

Early the next morning, she was back with the two giggly girls—the ones I had mentally dismissed under the coconut tree two days ago.

"They want to learn, too," she explained.

I gulped in dismay, thinking, *The "important, prestigious" men....*

Reluctantly, I put primers into their hands and demonstrated how to turn pages. The girls learned quickly, going through the primer faster than I dreamed possible. Their enthusiasm spurred me on to preparing Primer II, and then III. After three months, the girls could read anything I stuck in front of their noses.

One Sunday afternoon, Jim and I strolled to the village. A huge crowd stood in front of Sonalu's house staring down at something, but we couldn't see what. The silence was overwhelming.

Feeling anxious, I nudged my way through the crowd with Jim close behind. When we reached the center we saw what captured the stunned, silent crowd. There, on a large banana leaf, sat three girls reading aloud from Jim's rough draft, handwritten portion of Genesis, pretending not to notice they had the attention of the entire village.

I looked around at the crowd. They wore expressions of profound wonder and respect. Then I caught a glimpse of Binny with his head cocked to one side, his mouth gaping.

I stood there thinking how just a few months back the girls hadn't known how to hold a book, yet here they were reading God's Word to everybody. A shiver crept up my spine.

Swallowing at the huge lump in my throat, I knew I could never give up and go home. The satisfaction God gave me at that moment was worth far more than a soft couch, or anything else home could offer.

After the girls finished reading, everybody wanted to touch the paper containing their talk. Several noticed Jim and me standing nearby and, with hopeful smiles, approached us.

"Will you teach me to count words, too?" they wanted to know. I saw Binny coming. He greeted me shyly and asked if he could come to school. The entire crowd seemed to engulf us. They all wanted to come to school, even men too old to see well were promising not to be remiss in their attendance.

Amidst the stream of people, I caught Jim's eye and remarked: "Not a soul is asking for payment, did you notice?"

"No one's asked me for a shirt yet," he said with a wink—"or salt."

The next day Jim built a small shelter in front of the house where I could hold classes. A men's class started immediately, followed by a young women's class. As I taught the men, problems surfaced that I had not encountered while teaching Sonalu or the two girls. For one thing, they did not seem to be excited about learning.

At 6:30 in the morning, I rang the bell hoping the men would learn that if they came early to class, they would still have plenty of time to work in the gardens afterwards. But time meant nothing to the men, and they sat in their houses talking and chewing betelnut till well after 7:00. It irked me to see the ladies, who always arrived early, wait almost an hour for the men to finish.

Another thing, the men were not quick to learn. A few of the older ones took agonizingly long to read one sentence. Using a pig spear as a pointer, I taught from a large syllable chart at the front of the room. But the older men would forget the syllables they had learned and guess the wrong answer every time.

The fast readers got impatient and would blurt out the correct answers. As a result, the slower readers got worse, relying on someone else to tell them the answers. "You're stupid!" the faster ones would finally say. "You'll never learn!"

I tried to be strict and glared at anyone who talked out of turn. Some days my patience grew thin, and I wanted to whack all of them over their heads, tie them up and press the point of my spear into their hearts till the slow readers promised not to guess at syllables and the fast readers not to speak out of turn.

Isoro was the worst offender. He never missed a chance to taunt his brother Hwi'ura, the oldest in the class. Whenever the stammering, insecure man would make a mistake, Isoro would sigh heavily. *Should I—a woman—send Isoro—an intelligent and respected man—out of class? In this culture it wouldn't be right*. I battled daily to hold my tongue.

"You horse!" he blurted out to his older brother one day. Isoro had never seen a horse before, nor had anyone else in the village, but "You horse!" was the going cliché among the younger set. They used it when they were angry as well as when they were enthusiastic. Isoro reasoned that if there were such a thing as a horse, Hwi'ura must be it.

Embarrassed by his brother's inabilities, Isoro asked in disgust, "Why do you come to school? Your head is so hard that nothing will ever get inside!"

That did it! "Isoro!" I exclaimed, feeling the adrenalin pumping through my veins, the heat rising to my face. "You get up and leave right now!"

The younger brother looked at me as though he hadn't quite heard correctly. "Go!" I demanded. The room seemed to sway in an uneasy silence. Isoro arrogantly turned his head to one side and sniffed—the Managalasi way to ignore a person and at the same time, feign indifference.

There he sat, the bulk of his torso leaning stubborn-like against the middle post of the lean-to. He wasn't going anywhere. Oddly enough, I felt relieved. I didn't want him to leave. Next to Chululu, Isoro was the best I had. Suppose he never came back?

The sulking figure remained quiet while I helped his brother stutter painfully through the syllable chart. It was hard on all of us, and I was glad when the class came to an end. Then I called the six women who waited eagerly on the porch. They quickly spit out their betelnut, and shuffled over to the classroom.

I tried not to reveal that Chipi, the youngest, was my favorite. On our first day of class, the pretty pre-teen learned to read and write four syllables. I watched her expression as she put the syllables "a" and "mo" together and read "amo," the word for "father." Her face lit up like the sun. Next she did the same with "ka" and "mo," then read the complete sentence, "Amo kamo" (Father sees).

As she continued reading about the things Father could see, it struck her like a clap of thunder—she was reading Managalasi words! Her fascinated eyes grew larger with every word, and once in a while she glanced up at me with a smile that spread from ear to ear. My joy matched hers, and I realized there couldn't be enough money from any job in the States to equal the wealth I received from helping Chipi learn to read her language. This was satisfaction beyond money.

Section Two

The Early Light of Dawn

The Early Light of Dawn

Today was the day. The Cessna would be coming from Ukarumpa to pick us up and fly us back to the center of operations. At the center we would receive mail regularly. We could use toilets that flushed, shop at the base store, drink water that ran from a faucet, and best of all—communicate with people who spoke English. Joyful thoughts of seeing friends again set butterflies working a frenzy in my stomach.

While at Ukarumpa, we would write a technical paper describing the Managalasi alphabet. Eunice Pike, a phonology specialist, arrived at Ukarumpa from the States to help us and other teams write these descriptive papers.

Also while at Ukarumpa, we would prepare for the birth of our first child. I was seven months pregnant, and Jim and I were excited about becoming parents.

Our village friends sat everywhere, on the porch, the lawn, and alongside the path, waiting to say good-bye. A few older ones had tears in their eyes. Their sadness touched me, yet I felt a happiness because they cared enough to want us to stay. As anxious as I was to go, a part of me wanted to remain with the old people. Could it be I was learning to care for these strangers who weren't my people? Maybe even to **love** them?

Avami sat on the ground by the trail chewing betelnut and coughing. "Mother, ese," I said, taking her thin hand in mine. There was no smile on her face, and her eyes avoided mine. I knew she wanted me to stay.

"Ese, my daughter," she said without looking up, then began a coughing spasm. I wanted to hug her good-bye and tell her I would miss her, but not having seen anyone in this culture give hugs, I refrained. And I didn't know how to convey "missing a person" in their language yet.

A small huddle of Managalasis watched me as I started up the trail for the airstrip. They held their arms out limply, and I shook hands with each of them. Sonalu's mother, Hucharu, sat beside the trail farther up. "Jaki-ooo," she wailed loudly, then "Jimi-eeey."

More wailing came from behind me. I knew it was Avami. Sonalu caught up with me and snatched the purse from my hand to carry for me.

"Why are they crying?" I asked her.

"The people think you and Jim won't come back."

"Why not?"

"They say you won't bring your baby here to live with us; our place is too dirty. They say you will live in a strong house, a house with an iron roof. Our village is not good enough." I saw the deepening concern on her face as she conveyed these thoughts to me.

"Tell them we are coming back with our baby to live here. I'll write you a letter and tell you when the plane will bring us. Come to the airstrip on that day and wait for us," I said, trying to reassure her.

A smile lit up Sonalu's face. "I'll make a stringbag for your baby and carry him for you. He'll be just like our Managalasi babies."

The thought of my baby snuggled in a stringbag like their babies brought a grin to my face. Then I wondered what Mom would think about her grandchild in a stringbag, suspended from a tree instead of tucked in a proper crib with clean sheets and ruffles.

It was almost noon, and the sun was hot. Sonalu whipped out her knife and cut a stalk of sugarcane into bite-sized pieces. Thankfully, I ate each bite slowly as I climbed the long steep hill to the airstrip.

"The plane is coming...the plane is coming," the people said, long before I could hear or see anything. Then, sure enough, I heard the humming sound. Happiness rippled through my body.

James Vincent Baptista, climbing down from the pilot's seat, was a sight for sore eyes. He would never know the depth of my gratitude for his skill as a pilot and for his part in our work at Numba Village. Without James to fly us to and from our village, we would not be able to give God's Word to the Managalasis.

James noticed my maternity dress and yelled, "Hey, Judy! I like your 'uniform'!"

Hearing my American name, I cringed. "James," I said reaching out to grasp his hand in welcome. "You have to call me 'Jaki' now."

"Jaki?" he exclaimed as his forehead wrinkled. "Why do I have to call you 'Jaki'?"

Quickly I explained, and James' face changed from puzzlement to amazement. Then he laughed. "You wouldn't read about that," he said, using his favorite expression. He began putting our cargo into the belly of the plane, still shaking his head.

Isai would accompany us to Ukarumpa to help with language work. Because of his extreme shyness, we knew he would get homesick, so we asked his friend Taiva to come too. Leaving their homes and riding in an airplane for the first time must have been traumatic, for when it was time to board, I detected fear in their eyes.

"Taiva, ese, Isai, ese!" the people were saying. Without looking back or responding, the boys climbed into the plane and sat like two wooden statues as Jim buckled their seatbelts. Isai sat in back near the luggage, and I slid in next to Taiva. When the engine whirred to life, Taiva clasped the armrests and shut his eyes tightly, as if in physical pain.

"Taiva," I called. No response. I shook his arm, but he refused to open his eyes or let go of the armrests. "Say 'ese' to your people!" I yelled loudly so he would hear above the engine's roar, but the frightened boy would not budge.

Crowds lined the sides of the airstrip. "Esa'ua!" I mouthed, and waved frantically as we rolled by. Seconds later we were airborne. I turned around to check on Isai. As I expected, he looked nervous, but managed to muster courage enough to look out the window.

"Taiva!" I yelled, trying once more to get a response. Taiva sat stiffly in his seat, like a man about to be electrocuted.

"Look! There's Mt. Lamington. We're going right by it." Taiva's eyelids flickered open for less than a second, then squeezed shut. He sat in the same position until we landed at Ukarumpa, one and a half hours later.

I had forgotten how cold it could get on the SIL base at the center. At 5,200 feet, the air nipped at our unacclimated bodies. The boys shivered to the point of illness. They were used to 90 degree weather. At Ukarumpa, the temperature sometimes dipped to 40 degrees in the evenings.

A large blue and white van took us directly to the center store where we bought them shirts, pants, blankets and sweatshirts. Next we bought several cans of fish, meat and bags of rice.

Ukarumpa, SIL's center of operations.

After we took the boys to their living quarters, Isai said, "We can't eat any meat or fish."

"Why not?" Jim asked, surprised.

"Because our relatives back in the village don't have any meat or fish, and we feel too sad to have so much."

"You'll be hungry," Jim warned, and we left them rubbing their hands before a crackling fire.

On our first evening at the center, the Wiggers family invited us to eat in their home. Ken, a pilot, and Pat, who worked in the center post office, were friends we met during our field orientation course in Mexico a few years prior. Being support personnel, they lived on the center year round.

Pat's smile welcomed us at the door. Other friends were also invited. We talked nonstop for hours. It was as though six months of talk and laughter had built up inside me and now, like Mt. Lamington, it had erupted and was flowing out.

As we ate fresh meat and homemade biscuits, I enviously looked around Pat's house. The walls and furniture looked so clean and shiny—no soot smears anywhere. The polished wood floor had no cracks for mice to creep in and out of, nor did it shake unsteadily when walked on. Best of all, Ken had installed a flush toilet along with a shower and sink. No trekking out with a flashlight on rainy nights to a cold outhouse.

Then Pat served the dessert—angel food cake with ice cream, Hershey's syrup and walnuts sprinkled on top. I was in fantasy land. With the edge of my fork I cut off a piece of cake and placed it in my mouth. "Ohhhh," I moaned aloud, and everybody turned my way. Then, tongue-in-cheek I asked, "Why didn't I marry a pilot instead of a translator?" and watched the expressions on the faces of my friends—at first stunned, then broken up with convulsive laughter. We talked and laughed until almost midnight.

I was so thankful for a center where we could get a break from village living, and thankful for friends who provided the laughter, the caring and sharing I needed—the best medicine for me.

When I got out of bed the next morning, the floor felt like ice beneath my feet. Shuffling through the box, I quickly pulled out a pair of socks to wear. The air felt brisk, reminding me of autumn back in New Jersey. After breakfast, Jim gathered our language materials, and we set out to meet with Eunice Pike for our language session.

After one hour we discovered the Managalasi language had three syllable patterns. Next, Eunice showed me how to line up my material to check on the stress patterns, and our first session ended.

Encouraged, Jim and I went home to work with the boys. We drilled them over and over on every word in our file. After a few hours, all the words started to sound the same. We couldn't hear which syllable the stress fell on.

I kept reminding myself that doing such tedious work was important. To have a good translation of God's Word, we had to understand how the alphabet system worked.

Soon, Isai began shifting uneasily in his chair. Taiva's yawns grew louder and more frequent.

"Let's take a break!" Jim suggested.

"We can't! We don't have enough contrasts yet, and what we do have, we're not sure of."

Jim looked at me and shook his head in disagreement. "The boys are tired. Let's take a walk to the store and work again later."

The boys had already jumped out of their chairs. They outnumbered me. As we walked along the dirt road, I asked Jim, "What if we still can't hear where the stress falls by 9 o'clock tomorrow morning? Miss Pike will wonder how we ever got into Wycliffe."

"Can your students read the primers you wrote?" he asked. I knew he was trying to make a point.

"Yeah," I said, more like a question than a statement.

"And can they read the verses in Genesis that Isai and I translated?"

I nodded.

"Well, that's got to prove we know something."

Eunice was pleased with the work we showed her the next morning. I was walking on air. Next we had to work on Managalasi phrases. Do some words drop out in phrases? Are some letters lost? What happens to the stress when you say a phrase?

Again we concentrated hard on these areas, then did the same with sentences and finally paragraphs. After many stress headaches Jim and I got our phonology paper written. But it would not have been completed nearly as fast without the help of Eunice Pike. How thankful we were for her willingness to put aside her own projects for a while to help us with ours.

Each day I walked to the printshop at the far end of the base to work on the layout of our primers. Soon they would be real books instead of handmade pages. Jim worked on analyzing the grammar and, for a break, a little translation.

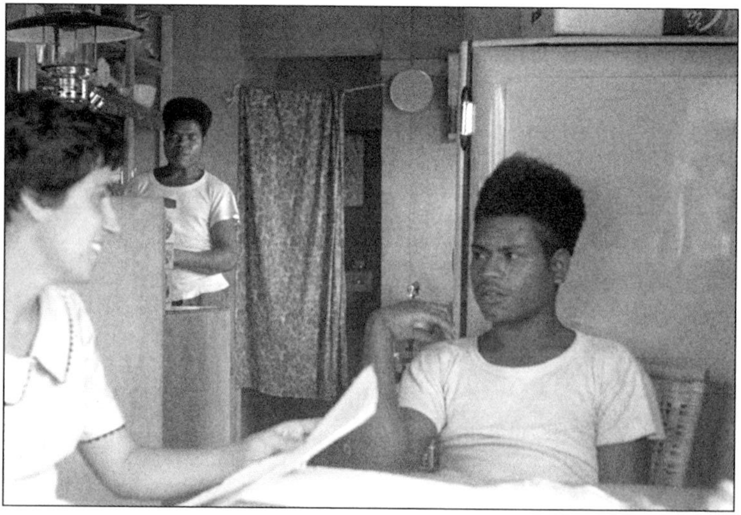

Isai helps establish an alphabet for his language.

For months, Jim had searched for a word to express "love." The closest equivalent he found meant "to like" or "to want," but these words were not strong enough to show the depth of God's love. Jim did not know how to dig deeper to find this all-important word. Friends who prayed for us knew about the struggle, and many prayers went up.

As we were eating lunch one day, Taiva brought in a letter from his girlfriend. Wasapi, one of my better students, had completed the reading course and she had written the letter. Taiva, however, had not learned to read yet.

The lovesick boy sat down on the floor in front of me as I read his language to him. Jim stopped eating and listened. Wasapi told some village news, then boldly expressed how she missed him.

"The days all seem like night since you left," she wrote. "Every day is dark. I cry huge tears for you. I give you my heart. Wasapi."

"Read that last sentence again!" Jim said.

"I give you my heart," I read.

Jim looked at Taiva. "Taiva, when do you tell someone you give them your heart?"

Taiva looked embarrassed. He started to reply, then stopped. Finally, he shrugged and said, "When boys and girls are courting, they say that."

"Do parents say that to their children?" Jim asked.

"Of course. Everyone gives their heart to their children."

"That's it!" Jim exclaimed, as though he had found the pot of gold at the end of the rainbow. "That's the expression for 'I love you.'"

It was a phrase that would make the familiar "For God so loved the world that He gave His only Son...." spring to life in their language. Jim could now translate John 3:16 with confidence that they would understand how much God loved them.

Two weeks before my due date, we flew to Lae, a beautiful town with tropical trees, plants and flowers beside the roadsides. A hospital staffed by Australian and Papua New Guinean doctors and nurses sat on a hillside overlooking Lae's international airport.

I loved Lae where rain pelted down every night and the air smelled fresh the next morning beneath the tropical sun's rays. Driving down the main road was one of my favorite things to do. Huge trees grew on both sides of the street, their thick branches arched overhead till they met in the middle. Driving beneath was like moving through a lush green tunnel.

Taiva and Isai quickly located Managalasi boys from other villages who worked in Lae. These boys spoke a slightly different dialect. One day Taiva and Isai came to the apartment where we stayed and relayed a message the other Managalasis had received via the grapevine.

"A woman has died," Taiva said.

"Who? From where?" we asked.

"Avami, your mother, died last week," he finished sadly.

My heart felt like a stone in my chest. "How did she die?" I asked, not wanting to believe what I was hearing.

"She got a big sick and died," was his only explanation.

Thoughts of the last day I saw her sitting on the ground in front of our house rushed to my brain. *I didn't tell her I would miss her,* I thought. *I didn't hug her good-bye. I didn't say, "Wato, I give you my heart."* But worse than anything, my village mother died without knowing that Jesus, the Son of God, died for her sins. Trying to keep the tears in check, I conveyed my feelings to Jim.

"That's why we've got to learn the language as fast as we can, so that no more of our friends will die before they hear about the Lord," Jim replied.

Thoughts of where Avami was spending eternity darkened my days. I tried to imagine living in the village without her. I had lost my desire to return to Numba and Sivurani, but I knew I had to keep my promise to Sonalu...and the village people.

Some of those shadows lifted on February 5th—the day our son Rick was born. After I was returned to my hospital room, Jim stood by my bedside and took my hand in his. Lights, like two bright stars, shone from his eyes, and he looked happier than I had ever seen him. Even though previously Jim said it didn't matter if it were a girl or boy, I knew deep in his heart he wanted a son. And the Lord granted him that wish.

We flew back to Ukarumpa for a few weeks to wait for my full recovery. One day, my friend Joice Franklin who had just returned from her furlough with her husband, Karl, stopped by with some baby clothes for Rick.

"We visited Lucy during a stop in New Jersey," she told me.

"What! You saw Mom?" I was incredulous.

"Yes, she told us your good news. Karl and I were thrilled."

"I can't believe you spent time with my mother—in our house!"

"We had a wonderful visit, but couldn't waste a minute—we just had to go shopping for the baby."

No other friend could cheer me quite like Joice. She was my encourager, and I shared some of my feelings about not wanting to go back to the village—ever.

"Don't worry about that," she said quickly. "I felt the same way after our first time with the Usa people. There are so many new things to adjust to, and it's difficult. The first time out is the hardest. It gets easier and easier. You'll see."

I pondered those words as Jim and I packed to go back to the village. I hoped Joice was right. One thing I did know for sure. Things couldn't be much worse than they had been the first time.

Did Sonalu get my letter in time? I wondered as we flew over majestic mountaintops back to our village home. Baby Rick, wrapped in a new blue blanket, slept soundly to the steady hum of the engine. *I hope she'll be there.*

Ken Wiggers circled the airstrip and looked back at me from the pilot's seat. "Looks like you'll have enough people to help carry cargo." His smile was encouraging.

Since neither Isai nor Taiva had ever been away from their village before, three months had been a long time. I turned to check the expressions on their faces. Isai struggled not to show any emotion, but Taiva, with happiness written all over his face, smiled big enough for both of them.

I looked down at masses of people, and my heart turned over—Sonalu had received my letter and had spread the word.

After the plane bumped to a standstill, Jim hopped out and heaved open the door. As I stepped from the plane, Rick cradled in my arms, I looked up into what seemed like a thousand faces saying, "Weeee, wheyyyy," in amazement. People whom I'd never seen before were craning their necks for a first glimpse at a white-skinned baby.

Arms and hands streaked with perspiration and grime, reached out to hold my brand new, spanking clean baby. A shudder of alarm rippled through my body as I realized I did not want these people to touch my baby. What if he got their germs and became sick? Suppressing my horror, I looked at Jim with a "What should I do?" look.

"Let those old women hold him," he urged. "A little dirt's not gonna hurt him."

"But he might get sick from germs," I countered.

"You can't worry about his getting sick or dirty. If you keep the baby from these people, it'll put up a wall between us and them. This is a time when you totally have to trust God to take care of him." With that, he went back to help Ken.

As Jim and Ken unloaded the plane, I watched my son being passed from person to person. I silently committed little Ricky's health to God. I examined the crowd and saw a lot of old folks. My heart melted. Some of these people looked too old to breathe, yet they traipsed miles over mountains to see the white man's baby.

Koranoma, an older man from Numba Village, held Rick out at arm's length to inspect his face. "His nose is wide, like our noses," he declared. I moved over next to the older man to examine my son's nose.

"It's because you and Jim have been eating our yams. That's why he has a Managalasi nose instead of an American nose," he explained. The crowd bubbled with excitement, nodding their heads.

"What's his name?" several asked at once.

"Ricky," I said and watched heads turn like wheat swaying gently in the wind as Rick's name passed across the lips of every bystander.

Then I heard the words "take off" coming from several people. Some of them looked directly at me and repeated the words, while others spoke to Sonalu. "Tell Jaki," I heard them say.

Sonalu put her chin down on her chest and approached me with an odd smile on her face. She didn't speak right away so I asked her what they said.

Sonalu hesitated, then explained slowly, "Everybody thinks your baby is different from our babies because his skin is white. They want you to take his clothes off so they can see if he's human like their babies or if he's different."

Their concept knocked me for a loop. Stunned, I began to unsnap the stretch outfit I dressed Rick in, hours before. He screamed the whole time I unwrapped him. Clusters of Managalasis closed in, gawking. When his diaper came off, the multitude cried, "Wheeeee! He's a human being! He's a human being!" Everyone appeared satisfied, and I quickly diapered him again.

Ken, ready to fly back to Ukarumpa, was shaking our hands good-bye. Watching the plane take off brought tears to my eyes again. I hated to see that beautiful blue and white bird go; it was like cutting off the link that connected me to civilization.

Sonalu stood beside me. She handed me the new stringbag she had woven for Rick. "I'll carry him for you," she said with a proud smile. Numbly, I stood by watching Sonalu put Rick into his new bed. In one full sweep, she lifted him in the stringbag, placed the handle on her woolly head and started toward the base of the mountain. Rick stopped crying immediately. Grateful, I followed behind.

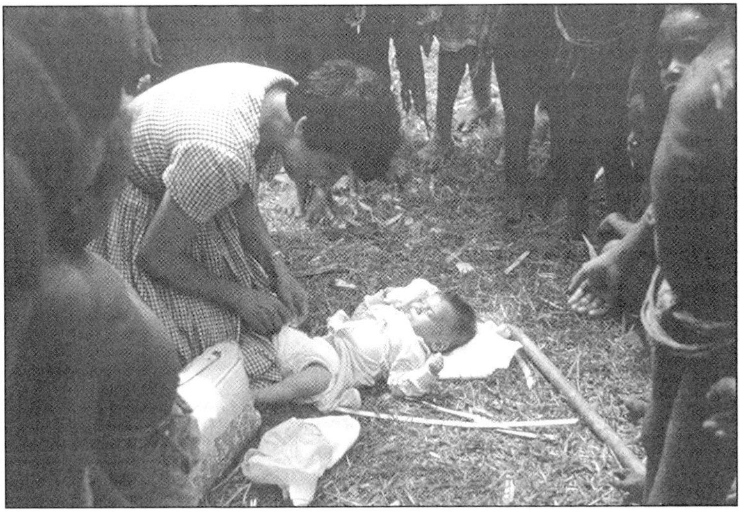

"Is he like our babies?" the Managalasis wondered about Rick.

The next morning, Jim was on the roof securing a huge yellow tarp onto the rafters. He told me that rainwater would run off the tarp into the long bamboo he rigged up as guttering and collect in the two forty-four gallon drums. Jim already had the pipes fitted into the drums and extending inside to the kitchen where he installed a sink.

Jim tied a tarp to the roof of our house to collect rain water.

Having a baby in the house seemed to soften the feelings of the Numba people towards us, for now they visited almost as often as our Sivurani friends. One day, as I was bathing Rick in a large plastic basin, Koranoma walked cautiously into the kitchen. As I turned to greet him, his mouth dropped open and the muscles in his neck tensed. "You shouldn't wash your baby!" he blurted out. "The spirits don't like that. They'll bite him, and he'll die."

"No, Koranoma," I said gently, hoping the smile on my face would convey I had no fear. "I wash Ricky everyday. Look at him! He's not sick and he's not dying."

Koranoma looked down at Rick enjoying his bath. "Besides," I added, enunciating each word of my simple Managalasi to be sure the older man would understand. "God who lives above the sky takes care of my baby. The spirits cannot bite him."

After I wrapped Rick in a towel, I handed him to the awe-struck visitor to hold while I poured out the bath water. Now Rick was ready for his nap.

"Bring him in here," I told Koranoma, and he followed me obediently into Rick's room. Jim had made a crib of sorts with bamboo and tied it together with vine. A piece of foam rubber served as a mattress. "Put him down here," I said, pointing to the crib. After the man gently laid Rick in his bed, he looked around the room. "Where do you and Jim sleep?"

Pointing to the adjacent room I said, "In there."

An incredulous look swept over the man's face. "No! No! You and Jim must put your bed down in here, next to your son's bed. If he's all alone, the spirits will come in the night and bite him. He'll die!"

"Come," I said, beckoning with my hand. As we walked back to the kitchen, I repeated what I told him during Rick's bath. "God takes care of us every day and every night. We are not afraid. The spirits cannot bite us."

"I'm going now," he said, the fearful, unbelieving look still on his face. "Ese."

"Koranoma, ese," I replied, then went outside to check on Jim. He had finished tying the tarp to the roof and was on his way down. "Now, all we need is a good rainfall, and we'll have running water in the house," he said, wiping the sweat from his brow. "It's such a beautiful day, let's get the camera and take some pictures of Rick with the people."

"Okay," I said. "Let me see if he's asleep." Rick was lying on his bed gurgling happily, and I picked him up. Jim got the Polaroid and we headed toward Sivurani Village. We passed some women on the trail. "Why are you carrying your baby in your arms?" they asked.

"This is the way American people carry their babies," I explained.

"Americans are ignorant," one woman remarked. "Carrying babies that way makes your arms ache. You should carry your son in a stringbag on your head."

"But my hair is like the threads that grow on corn—slippery, and the stringbag will slide off."

The women seemed satisfied with that, and, as Jim and I continued on, I could hear them discussing my "slippery" hair.

When we arrived at the village, we went first to Inao's house. He crouched before the embers of last night's fire. We greeted each other, and I put Rick into his arms. "Here's your grandson," I said. "I'm sorry Wato is not here to see him." Inao looked at me, shut his eyes and then opened them quickly, signifying "Yes" in their culture. I saw tears forming in the corners of his soft brown eyes. As we talked, Jim clicked a picture of the two of them.

Rick was often carried in a stringbag like Managalasi babies.

“The village talk is that you allow your son to sleep in a room by himself, yet the spirits don’t bite him,” my village father said, unaware that Jim had taken the photo.

“Hey, Jaki!” a woman’s voice shouted, interrupting our conversation. “Come over to my house with your baby!”

“No!” another shouted. “Come to my house!”

“Wait! I’m coming soon.” I shouted back as several others ambled over to Inao’s house. Returning my attention to my sad, village father, I replied: “That’s true, Father. Rick sleeps alone. God takes care of him while we sleep.”

Presto! The picture came sliding out of the camera and, after inspecting the photo, I passed it to Father.

Inao stared at a miracle.

“You shouldn’t take pictures of your baby!” he said, horrified. “You are taking his spirit away from him. Your son won’t grow up to be a man. He’ll stay small all his life—like a dwarf!”

“Let me see! Let me see!” the bystanders were saying. After looking at the photo, the others agreed. “Don’t take any more pictures. Your son will be a dwarf!”

“God takes care of Rick,” we repeated. “He’ll grow tall like Jim,” I said.

We visited each house in the oval-shaped village, Jim snapping pictures of Rick with his Managalasi family. For those who would have eyes to see, evidence was emerging which would poke holes in the darkness of their ancient beliefs.

On the way home I said to Jim, “Did you notice how everybody wants us to visit with them in their homes now that we have a baby?”

"Being a mother is one thing you can do just as well as these women," Jim said and laughed. "It'll help them relate to you better."

I had to agree. "And to think I worried about having a baby in the middle of nowhere, and with no relatives, especially grandparents close-by. It looks like every person in both villages will be a relative of some kind to Ricky."

"And he'll have more grandparents than ever," Jim said, patting the baby on the back as we walked.

Just as we got to the house, a young man came up to us with a packet of mail. Excited, I ripped it open, scanning for letters from Mom. Sure enough, there were a few aerograms with her familiar handwriting.

"Dear Jim, Jude, and my baby chickadee," one letter started out. "I'm coming to New Guinea! Dad's afraid I'm going to get eaten by cannibals, but I'm coming. I've got to see my first grandson!"

I couldn't believe what I was reading—Mom...coming here. Overcome with emotion, I felt like a cup—the cup the Bible describes as full and running over with joy.

As soon as it was light enough to see, I sprang out of bed and picked up my sleeping baby. "Today is the day you're going to meet your grandmother," I told Rick happily, trying to keep my excitement in check. I glanced at my watch. In three hours Mom would be arriving with my friend, Betty Baptista, James' wife, to visit us for six weeks.

I fed and bathed Rick, then handed him to Sonalu and sent her on ahead to the airstrip. Jim organized carriers to fetch water so there would be plenty for showers afterwards. After cutting up fresh pineapple and papaya, I zipped out of the house and caught up with Sonalu.

She waited for me just before the cemetery where several great warriors were buried. Their earthly achievements made them powerful spirits today, and no one dared walk past the cemetery alone.

"Don't be afraid of those dead people," I said, as we strode past the much-feared plots. "They died many years ago, they can't hurt you."

Sonalu glanced fearfully toward the grave sites. "Their spirits walk around, and, if you're by yourself, they'll bite you," she said. "But when there's more than one person, they won't bite."

It bothered me that Sonalu, and everybody else, believed Satan's lies so strongly, but, still limited in what I could say, my only reply was, "There are no spirits walking around. These people are dead and cannot bite."

Rick slept on as we trudged uphill to the airstrip. When we reached the cargo shed at the top of the strip, Sonalu removed the stringbag with Rick still asleep inside and hung it carefully on an exposed nail.

At the first buzz of the plane's approaching, I swallowed hard. Two and a half years had passed since I'd last seen Mom, but her frequent letters kept us up to date. As the plane circled for the landing, my chin quivered, and I could no longer swallow.

"Jaki's about to cry, Jaki's about to cry," a younger girl exclaimed in a sing-song tone. Sonalu shushed her.

The plane touched down, rolled to the top of the strip, spun around next to the cargo shed and halted. I could feel my heart beat faster, my eyes brimming over with tears. Mom's face appeared in the window. I tried to smile but couldn't. Moving close to the side of the plane, I reached out to touch the window where she sat and saw that Mom was crying too. Jim whipped open the doors and began unbuckling her seat belt. The next moment, we were hugging each other and crying.

"I thought I'd never get here," she said, wiping her eyes with a tissue. "The trip was so-o-o long. You look wonderful. How are you, honey?"

It took me a few seconds to answer. "Great!...now," I choked. Jim helped Betty down from the front seat and she, having learned the Managalasi greeting beforehand, yelled out, "Jaki, ese!"

"Ese, Betty," I replied, giving her a welcome hug.

"Where's the baby?" Mom asked suddenly, as if just remembering the purpose of her trip.

"Oh, Rick's asleep in there," I said, pointing to the stringbag that swayed slightly in the breeze.

Mom's head snapped back first to me, then Jim, then back to me again. "WHAT?" she gasped. "My grandson is in that sack? Hanging from a nail?" The indignant look on her face made Jim and me laugh like we hadn't laughed since our first evening at Ukarumpa. Jim fetched Rick from the stringbag, jolting him from a sound sleep. He screamed loudly as Jim carried him over and placed him in his grandmother's arms.

"There, there," Mom said soothingly with a loving smile. "Grandma's here to take care of you. Everything's gonna be all right." Rick continued to scream as she rocked him tenderly in her arms.

As soon as the boxes and suitcases were assigned carriers, we started on the trek home, a trek that would take longer than the plane ride from Ukarumpa to here, but I didn't tell Mom that.

Betty, a good hiker and full of energy, plunged on ahead with Jim while I walked at a snail's pace beside Mom. Seeing how well Rick settled in his stringbag on Sonalu's head, Mom realized the bag's value. "It's the most important possession for a woman here," I pointed out as we plodded between fields of long grass. Sonalu kept pace with us, wanting to know everything Mom said.

Betty had already taken her shower when we finally trailed in. Jim carried hot water into the shower room for Mom where she was introduced to the bucket shower. "What a wonderful idea," she exclaimed.

I was pouring coffee when Mom finished showering. "Wait," she cried, going to her suitcase. "I brought something I know you like to eat with your coffee." She came back to the table with my favorite candy.

"Candy bars!" I yelled ecstatically, ripping off the wrapper. Jim took one and passed another to Betty. After removing the paper, we noticed the outside layer of chocolate was discolored and moved slightly. The chocolate had probably gone bad in the heat of the long trip. Wordlessly, Betty put hers aside, but Jim and I began picking out worms.

"What are you doing?" Mom asked with alarm. "Do they have worms?" I shook my head so as not to concern her and bit off a third of the bar. "No!" she howled in alarm. "Don't eat those! Oh," she gasped. "You can't eat candy that had worms in it. You'll get sick!"

Jim swallowed half a bar and looked at Mom with a glimmer of amusement in his eyes. "Oh, you kids!" was all she could manage to say. We were used to picking flies out of milk and bugs from rice and other foods, so candy with worms didn't trouble us in the least. The look on Mom's face made it impossible to hold back our laughter any longer. Mom scrutinized the three of us as we wiped tears from our eyes. She didn't crack a smile, making it all the funnier. "I give up," she said, pushing her chair back from the table. She went out onto the porch where dozens of Managalasis sat waiting for medicine. A crowd always gathered around 5:00 PM to have their cuts and bruises doctored.

Jim, Betty and I sat discussing Mom's reactions a while longer. Suddenly waves of yelling, like fans cheering in a baseball stadium, reached our ears followed by heavy footsteps trampling down the stairs. "What's goin' on?" Jim said, getting up from the table and hurrying to the front door. Betty and I jumped up and followed.

"Oh, no!" I heard Jim say as I pushed past him. I looked out onto the grass in front of the house and thought my eyes would pop from their sockets. Everyone had gathered around Mom, forming a tight circle so as not to miss anything. They wore incredible looks on their faces.

"Mom!" I yelled out in dismay, my Judeo-Christian background causing my stomach to tie up in knots. "What are you doing?"

"I'm doing the twist," she said, shimmying her hips from side to side. "It's a new dance that's popular at home right now." She continued to wiggle her body round and round, moving her arms up and down.

"Stop!" I cried, pushing my way to the center of the crowd and taking her arm. "You can't do the twist here!"

"Why not?" she challenged.

"Because in this culture women don't dance like that in front of men!"

"Look, everybody's enjoying themselves, laughing and having a good time," she replied, undismayed.

I jerked around and studied the faces of my brown friends. None seemed embarrassed or upset. Some men tried rotating their bodies, laughing at each other. Then Mom, with the smile of a cheshire cat, strutted to the porch, bounced up the stairs past Jim who still stood in the doorway, mortified.

Now it was Mom's turn to laugh at us.

Rainy days seemed sunny because Mom was here. She prepared meals and took care of Rick who cooed sweetly when she held him. Mom, bursting with pride, would gush, "You know your grandma now, don't you?"

Betty, an artist, illustrated the primers as I worked on new ones. She learned to say several phrases in Managalasi and tutored our village father in reading. Teaching Inao wasn't easy, as he hopelessly tried putting syllables together to make words. But Betty persisted, and Inao got through Primer I.

One morning Mitaura, Sonalu's cousin, brought bananas to sell. "Jim! Jude!" Mom cried, "Come see these bananas! They're the biggest I've ever seen!" Jim and I went out on the porch to take a look. Each banana looked big enough to make a complete meal.

"I didn't know how much I should pay him," Mom said.

Jim piped up, "I'll take care of it."

"At first we never paid with money," I explained to Mom. "These people wouldn't accept money because there was no place to spend it. Now we bring kerosene, matches, fish and salt from Ukarumpa for them to buy."

Mom had an amazed look on her face. "What did they do before you came?"

"They made their own salt and rubbed sticks together to make their fires, and...." I sniffed the air. "Hey! I smell paint!"

"Huh, where?" Jim responded, using a mock tone that told me he knew something I didn't. The paint fumes were coming from Mom's room, which would be our room later. I rushed to the front bedroom and found Betty painting the walls a beautiful salmon color. It made the greenery outside look even greener.

"Betty!" I cried, surprised. "How did the pilot ever allow paint on the airplane?"

"I had to pull some strings," she said with a sly smile. "And James packed it so it would be safe. BUT...don't tell anyone!"

"Of course not," I promised, not able to take my eyes away from the beautiful wall. To think my friend would smuggle in paint—for me. A warm happiness tingled over my body as I studied the wall. The splash of salmon would make a world of difference to our mouse-colored house.

At 5:00 o'clock that afternoon, the porch filled with people who needed medicine. Jim and I were training Morisi to wash sores with antiseptic and apply ointment so that one day he could take over this time-consuming job entirely.

This evening, I noticed Sonalu standing quietly to one side. *Why is she looking so sheepish?* I wondered. *Something's wrong*. I went over to her side.

"What happened?" I asked. Sonalu glanced up, brows furrowed, then quickly turned away. Her refusal to speak screamed that something was wrong. I kept after her till she told me.

"My cousin," she mumbled finally. "My cousin did bad to you."

"Who, Mitaura?" I asked, making sure I got the right person. When she nodded, I asked, "Why? What did he do?"

"While we were at the airstrip the other day, he stole your bananas." I looked to the area beyond our outhouse where we planted numerous banana trees. Sonalu continued. "Then my cousin came this morning and sold the bananas to you for money."

"What? You mean we bought our own bananas?" My tone was angry, and Sonalu looked down in shame. "It's okay," I said quickly, covering my anger. "It's not your fault."

"I'm sorry," she said sadly. "My cousin did no good."

At the dinner table I related the story to Jim, Mom and Betty. "Jim has fixed his lantern so many times," I lamented, "and we filled it with kerosene for free, just to help him out. And look what he does." I felt betrayed.

"That guy is some actor," Mom said. "He sure fooled me standing there with a sweet, innocent look on his face." Then she laughed boisterously. When her laughter reached a high tone, Betty and Jim laughed too. At first I didn't see the humor in it, but seeing them laughing so heartily helped me put the picture into perspective—us, buying our own bananas—what a joke!

Before dropping off to sleep that night, the words of an older missionary friend came to mind: "It's vital to have a sense of humor." Now I knew why.

"I could live in the village forever as long as Mom were here," I sighed as she dozed on the flight back to Ukarumpa. Of course this wasn't possible, and, after a two-week stay at Ukarumpa, Mom would return to New Jersey where Dad waited anxiously.

Jim sat in the back of the plane with Morisi, our medical helper, who would now assist us with language work at the center. Morisi's skin was as light as my Italian skin, and his ginger-colored hair set him apart from the rest. I turned around to see how he was traveling. He sat securely beside Jim with his usual pleasant smile. His quiet, serene nature caused him to appear innocent and trusting, but I knew better.

Every Saturday he would tell Jim, "Yes, I'm coming to Bible study tonight," but as soon as he saw Jim coming, he would sneak away into the woods. One day he got angry and knocked his mother to the ground. When I heard what he had done, I wrote him off as "no good," but Jim insisted he come with us. "Hope for the best," he told me.

The Center hostess had a letter waiting for us when we landed. Hooray! We would be staying in Karl and Joice Franklin's home, one of the nicest on the base. Mom's eyes brightened as we walked in the front door and saw the cozy, ruffled curtains at the windows. Word had spread, and it seemed like everyone living at Ukarumpa wanted to meet Lucy who did the "Twist" for the Managalasi people.

Alan Healey, an Australian linguist with two doctoral degrees, would be helping us with the Managalasi grammar. The thought of working with such an intellectual intimidated me. During our first meeting, Alan was kind. Yet, I knew it was difficult for him to use simple linguistic terms to accommodate our limited knowledge. Jim and I worked separately on different aspects of grammar and met with Alan in the afternoons. After I prepared the paradigms Alan suggested, he would look at the material and design charts to help us see the information easily.

"Aha!" he would say, like a detective discovering the missing clue. "Look at this!" Then he would proceed to show me how Managalasi words were strung together.

Each morning in a large auditorium, Jim and I listened to linguists give lectures on various phases of grammar. Most of what they said went over my head, and I sat on my chair like a mannequin in a storefront window.

One day Alan said, "Jaki, when you finish writing your grammar paper, I want you to give the lecture in the auditorium."

That moment was the closest I'd come to fainting. As soon as I collected my wits I asked, "Suppose someone asks me a question? What will I do?"

He laughed. "Just do the best you can. If you don't have the answer, I'll be there to help you."

I practiced giving my lecture like an Olympic hopeful. First, I lectured to Jim who encouraged me, then to Mom who, without understanding a word I said, nodded proudly back at me, then to baby Rick while he gurgled in his highchair, and finally to Jakanaka, our black cat. Then, I felt ready.

The day of my presentation arrived. I looked around the auditorium at the linguistic intellectuals and wondered why I had ever agreed to present the lecture. I must have been out of my mind, senseless, demented, stark-raving insane.

When Alan introduced me, everyone applauded. Embarrassed, I moved on legs of jelly to the front of the auditorium. I hoped the black skirt I wore didn't look too tight. Once I began, the words flowed naturally. After finishing, I sat down immediately, allowing no time for questions—I had no more light to shed on Managalasi verbs. Alan, with an understanding smile, stood and told a little more about the language, answering questions as he spoke.

I appreciated Alan Healey, not only for the tremendous knowledge he possessed, and not just for the fact that he never made me feel like the village idiot. I appreciated Alan because he willingly put aside his own translation work to help teams like Jim and me who lacked the ability to produce the grammar papers translators were required to write.

As I prayed thankfully for Alan, I became aware that he had just as much a part in the Managalasi New Testament as we did, and by helping so many, he would have more than one New Testament to present when he appeared before Christ one day.

One evening Vida Chenoweth, a professional marimbist, gave a concert in the meeting house. Mom, Jim and I, happy to be at Ukarumpa for the occasion, went early and sat down as close to the front as possible. I studied Vida as she stood at the front, the reddish highlights in her bobbed hair dancing beneath the fluorescent beams above. She stood poised behind her instrument, head bent forward, causing the sides of her short bob to hang in the exact place on both sides of her head. We sat enraptured for the next hour as music and artist became one with the audience.

I looked over at Mom a few times. "Vida plays with such feeling," Mom replied, wiping away her tears with the back of her hand.

Afterwards, we invited Vida to come for coffee. When she saw my copper coffee pot, she exclaimed, "Where did you get that? It's beautiful! I love it!" While she was admiring my coffee pot, an idea struck me. "Well," I said to her, "if you'll come out to our village and write hymns for the Managalasi people, I'll give you my coffee pot." As soon as the words were out, I was appalled. To think I would offer such a small reward for such an enormous task. I should have given her the pot without the conditions, I thought woefully.

"Hmmm," Vida murmured, as though considering what I suggested. I dared not hope. "That's what I came to New Guinea to do—write hymns for the different language groups. When do you want me to come?"

We flew with Mom to Lae where she would board a jet for the first leg of her journey home. "It won't be long now," she said at the airport, hugging me good-bye and planting soft kisses all over Rick's face. "The way the months fly by, you'll be home for your furlough in no time."

"Sure, Mom," I said, trying to smile. Rick would be two and a half. It seemed centuries away.

"And," Mom continued, giving Jim a hug, "when I go back home, I'm going to raise money for you to build your house at Ukarumpa."

"What?" I asked, surprised. "How?"

"I'm going to speak in churches and tell everybody what you and Jim are doing. I'll let them know you need a house and that the collection will go for your building materials."

Jim piped in. "It'll take a lot of money. We'll need at least $400 to start."

Six months after Mom left, the money came in and our house at Ukarumpa was completed.

"Don't worry about a thing!" Mom said with a confident grin. "All I have to do is tell them you eat candy with worms, and they'll dig deep into their pockets to help."

On our second night back in the village, Isai's aunt died. High-pitched wailing reached my ears, and oppression, fog-like, descended upon the village. People talked back and forth in whispers so as not to draw the attention of angry spirits to them.

A group of Isai's relatives sat beside the woman's still body swaying from side to side as they lamented. Their incantations were jumbled, first high pitched, then low. The house was swaying back and forth with them, and it seemed like the room was possessed by Satan himself.

I didn't want to enter the house, but Kiji, one of my favorite older friends, sat by the doorway and moved over to make room for Jim and me. I steeled myself, then, handing Ricky to Sonalu, slid in beside Kiji.

Isai's uncle held the dead woman's head in his lap. He bent over, put his mouth to her ear and yelled out her name. Cold chills ran up my back and down to my fingertips. "Get up!" he commanded harshly, as though he were angry at her for dying. "Ihiri, get up!" The air seemed electric.

When Isai took his turn crying, I felt disheartened. After listening to him for five minutes, I leaned over and whispered to Jim, "With everything you taught Isai about God, why is he behaving no differently than all the rest?"

"Because he's not a believer, that's why."

The small fire cast an eerie red glow in the room. The wailings continued, first imploring the dead woman to get up, then asking her why she left them, and finally beseeching her to come back. I didn't think I could bear it much longer, but Jim and I continued to sit stiffly in the semi-darkness. After Isai finished crying, his sister, Vurari, took his place. Vurari began to sob softly, then her cries grew louder. Soon she worked herself into a frenzy and was wailing out of control.

Sonalu reached inside the house and tapped me on the shoulder. "Ricky's hungry," she whispered, and thankfully I stepped down from the house. As Jim and I were about to leave, Isai approached Jim, his eyes cast downward. "Because my mother died, and now my father's sister, I have to help my father and work in the gardens everyday," he said.

Jim nodded with understanding. "Okay," he told Isai, "it would be good for you to help your father now."

Relief stretched across Isai's face and he looked at Jim through weary eyes. "Ese," he said awkwardly, and climbed back into the shadowy house with the ominous cries.

"Your language helper will be the first to become a Christian," other translators told us before we left the States. *Not in our situation,* I thought grimly, and wondered what we were doing wrong.

As we walked home, the sun's warmth felt good on my back and melted away the chill I felt from inside the house. "Who will help you now?" I asked Jim.

"Maybe I'll try Poki," he replied. "He's listened to Isai and me working together, so he has a good idea of what I'm after."

"Isn't he kind of young for such an important job?"

"I'll see. All he can do is try right now. At least until someone who's older and available comes along."

Sonalu helped me prepare my first Bible study for women. It would be in Tadedamara's house, just inside Sivurani. On the day of the study, I visited each home in both villages and invited all the women. "When you hear the conch shell," I said, "come to Tadedamara's house and I will teach you about the God who lives on top of the sky," I told them. Blank stares and unenthusiastic nods chipped away at my enthusiasm. *Would anyone come?* I wondered.

At 7:30 PM, I lit the lantern and walked up to Sivurani, going directly to Sonalu's house. I saw other women just getting home from their gardens. *They still have to build a fire and cook their husbands' food. Perhaps this is a bad time.*

Sonalu jumped down from her house, pushing the last of a purple yam into her mouth. "Jaki, ese," she said, through potato-crammed teeth. She took the conch shell from my hands and walked to the center of the village. She swallowed the yam and put her lips to a small hole. Then she blew on the shell with all her might, but no sound came. Sonalu laughed heartily. Undaunted, she tried again and this time with success. By the third blow, her result sounded as good as a man's.

"Will the women who live in Numba hear it too?" I asked.

"Mmmmm," my chubby friend responded in a high tone. "People who live across the valleys can hear," she said emphatically. "Long ago, when the men blew the conch shell, it meant the enemies were coming. People working in their gardens on the other side of the mountain would hear and come quickly."

We climbed into Tadedamara's house, and I hung my lamp on a rafter. The entire house—a cooking room and a small sleeping room—lit up. Despite a steady drizzle, eight women, some carrying babies, came to the first meeting.

"We're going to talk to God," I told them and unwrapped the paper that had my prayer written on it. "Close your eyes." The ladies stared back at me, as if they hadn't quite heard right.

Sonalu piped up, "Close your eyes and go to sleep while Jaki prays," she told them, using the same word the people used for talking to spirits. At first I though she was trying to be funny. I jerked my head up and looked around the circle of women, but everyone sat with eyes shut. I began to read my prayer. Two babies whimpered as I prayed, and the mothers talked aloud, not caring that they disturbed me and distracted everyone.

After praying, I began to teach from Mark's Gospel. My hope was to teach them a nugget about God, something simple that they could remember all week. The interruptions continued, giving me a good idea of what future Bible studies would be like.

After I finished the lesson, I started all over again, sentence by sentence. Then I had Sonalu repeat it all to be certain the women understood. When we finished, I expected some to have questions, but the women immediately began talking about mundane things like their work in the gardens, the weather, having backaches. Aamara mentioned having seen a snake. That started them off talking about snakes. I thought I heard one of them say the snake's spirit was in the sky. I asked Sonalu about it, and she explained that the rainbow in the sky is the shadow of a certain snake.

"No, no," I said emphatically. "God puts the rainbow in the sky after it rains." But I was not prepared to tell the story of Noah, so I said nothing more. Sonalu related to them what I had said. They avoided my stare, and some muttered. It was their way of saying, "Yeah, right!" I invited them to come again the next Thursday, and said good-night.

The next day, Jim verified this information with Poki. Yes, it was true. When this colorful snake slithered through the jungle after a rainfall, his shadow would appear in the sky.

As Jim worked on a trial translation of Genesis, Poki proved to be an excellent help. With each session he learned more about the God who created the heavens and the earth. One day he said to Jim, "I want this God to be my God." He and Jim prayed together, then Poki prayed for forgiveness of his sins and invited Jesus to come into his life. Jim and I were overjoyed. How wonderful it would be to have a true believer helping to translate the Scriptures.

Poki's decision gave me hope for the rest of the villagers. *When they understand like Poki does, they would choose the right God to be their God also.*

Music was woven into many aspects of Managalasi life including joy, mourning, dancing and working in the garden. Compositions told the history, and were passed from one generation to the next through song. We recorded all we could so we would be ready when Vida arrived. I waited for her at the house with fresh-cut fruit and heated water for a refreshing shower.

The slim musicologist stepped through the door in a crisp, plaid blouse and green corduroy skirt that wrapped around her waist and tied in the front. Just the slightest trace of perspiration beaded on her brow. "That's some hike!" she remarked and plopped down in the chair I offered.

"If it was so bad, why do you look like you just stepped out of a taxi cab?" I remarked. Vida laughed, and we drank lemonade while she informed Jim and me of the latest news from Ukarumpa. Then after her shower, she said, "I need as much quiet as possible so I can concentrate."

Quickly, I changed Ricky's diaper and handed him to Sonalu. "Take Ricky and all of the children sitting outside on the porch up to Sivurani," I instructed. "We have to have it quiet around here." Sonalu loved taking charge of Rick, and she looked like the Pied Piper going up the path with a herd of kids tagging behind.

Vida sat down at the dining room table with the tape recorder in front of her. She leaned forward with a serious look on her face as she listened intently to each song type. Amazed, I watched her write down musical chords, slurs, and triplets just like I would write down words when taking notes at a lecture.

After a few hours she asked, "Do you have the Gospel of Mark translated?"

Jim nodded.

"Let's start with Mark 16:15."

Jim shuffled papers to the verse in Managalasi: "Let go of your sins and believe God's Book," it read.

"Okay, Jaki, now I need to know where the stress falls on every syllable of every word in the verse."

Wasting no time, I underlined every stressed syllable with a red pencil. With that Vida proceeded to write the first hymn for the Managalasis, using their own musical patterns.

I studied her determined chin as she wrote each note on a music staff. Below the notes she wrote the words to Mark 16:15. Producing a small instrument that looked something like a harmonica, Vida played the melody for me.

"You have to teach this to your people," she told me matter-of-factly. My stomach did a somersault. "But I can't sing," I protested, aghast at the thought of performing in front of a group with so feeble a voice. "There's no way I can teach songs to our people. They'd laugh me to scorn."

"How about Jim, then?"

"Well, you can ask him, but that hillbilly of mine never learned when the pitch goes up or down."

Vida got the message and tried to encourage me. "Don't worry about the quality of your voice," she said. "You can practice and when you feel ready, we'll record the music and words on a short tape. We'll add their drum beat and shake the shakers in the background. Then you can just play the tape for your people to learn from."

I scratched my head, wondering how I could get out of such an ordeal. But the handwriting was on the wall—either I did this or it would not get done. I didn't want Vida's trip to be in vain.

"Come on," Vida coaxed. "I'll help you."

With misgivings, I agreed. My coach picked up her little instrument and played the first phrase. "Let go of your sins...." I sang out in high, thin anemic tones, then promptly burst into side-clutching laughter. Vida tried to restrain herself but soon joined me. For a few seconds, neither one of us could catch our breath long enough to say a word.

We tried again with the same result, only the laughter grew harder. I thought I would be sick. *How will I ever make it through a whole song?* I wondered. Several attempts had to be erased, and after two hours, I grew tired—too tired to laugh anymore. Vida was finally able to tape the entire song.

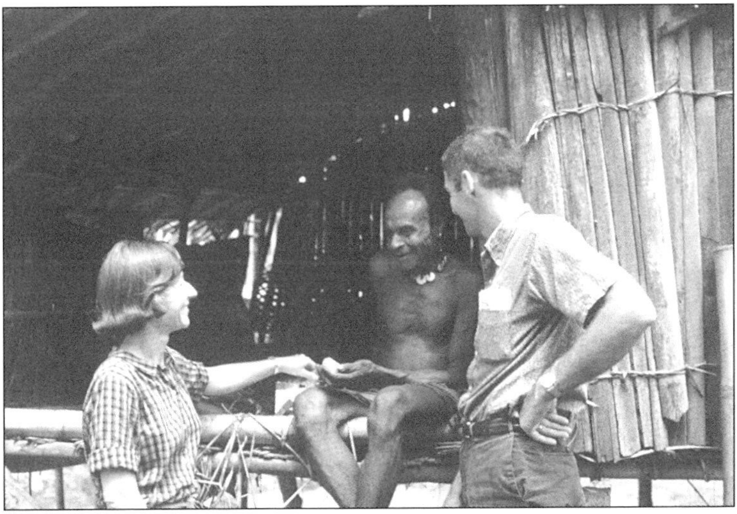

Vida analyzed the Managalasi music and composed hymns.

At Bible study that evening, Vida sat in one corner of the village house with the tape recorder propped on a cardboard box. She cut the tape so that when the song finished, it immediately began again. "The words and melody will sink into their subconscious minds, and they'll learn it faster," Vida explained, allowing the song to play over and over as the women crowded into Tadedamara's house. A new song was big news in the community, and almost all the women from both villages came. They did not want to miss out on anything. It was the biggest turnout yet.

On the bare, bamboo floor, beneath the glow of my small kerosene lantern, the women sat listening intently to the tape recorder. A small fire flickered cozily in the center of the room. When Vida turned off the recorder, I taught them phrase by phrase how to sing the tune. My voice cracked in a few places, and on the note that rose too high for my range, I whinnied like a horse and then my voice disappeared completely. I dared not look at Vida, but I could sense the rumbling of restrained laughter ready to erupt from deep inside her.

"Jaki's got a 'bad throat,'" Pupuri remarked in between phrases. There was no derision in her voice, yet her words stung. Ignoring the remark, I continued on, determined that these women learn the song that night.

Taking a short breather, I spoke silently to God. *You knew about this moment before I was born, Lord, and You could have equipped me a little better for the task. Why didn't You?*

After I taught the lesson, we sang the song a few more times. Some of the women had their rhythm instruments in their stringbags. They began shaking them in time to the song. Tadedamara took down her husband's drum from where it hung on the wall and began tapping it. The happy looks on the faces of the women told me they liked the song. With the shakers and drum it sounded like an authentic Managalasi song. Happiness tingled up and down both of my arms.

For a few moments, I sat in awe of God. I couldn't sing a lick, yet He used my weakness to accomplish something worthwhile. Feeling humbled, I glanced in Vida's direction.

"They're doing very well," Vida remarked above the singing and shakers. She looked pleased with their progress. How thankful I was at the moment that God sent Vida to our village so the Managalsis could sing hymns of praise to God in their very own style. And, at the same time, they were putting God's Word into their hearts. Even though singing the Scriptures would not make these women Christians, it was a start. I had confidence God would use these songs to bring the women to Himself when the time was right.

On the way home that night, I told Vida about the Managalsi explanation regarding the rainbow. "Does Jim have any of Genesis translated yet?" she asked.

"Yes, he and Poki have worked through twelve chapters."

"Good," she said. "Tomorrow I'll begin composing a song from the seventh and eighth chapters that will teach them why God put the rainbow in the sky."

On Sunday mornings, Poki began to teach the older people the things he was learning about God from his translation work with Jim. Everyone gathered at Ahmara's house. She was the oldest woman in the village and could not walk, so the others brought their mats to her house to sit on, while Poki taught at the foot of her stairway.

"And because Adam and Eve did bad," Poki taught one Sunday, "all of us are bad when we are born." Chief Ledu sat looking perplexed. After the Bible study finished, the chief cleared his throat loudly. Everyone sat quietly and waited for their leader to speak.

Poki taught the older people about God on Sunday mornings.

The chief paused, as if reflecting on what he had heard. He took another moment to enjoy his betelnut, then spit it out and wiped his mouth on his arm. Clearing his throat a second time, he began, "I'm not a bad man. I've never stolen anything from another person's garden; I don't get angry; I have only one wife; I'm not bad, I'm a good person."

At that, the group chimed in, "Yes, that's right," they agreed, reinforcing their chief's claim. "Ledu doesn't do any of those things, he's a good man."

Another piped up, "He never uses dirty talk either. He doesn't lie. He's been a good leader." All the men nodded in agreement.

Jim sat thinking about what to say. Managalasi law declared that if your wife could not bear children, it was admissible to leave her and take another. If anyone had the right to divorce his wife, it would be Ledu—his wife was barren, but Ledu did not do that. Instead, he chose to forfeit his right to children and remain faithful to his wife, amazing everyone. Without question,

Ledu was a model of integrity. Jim knew that it wasn't the time to dig deeply into the sin nature—these people did not have enough background to grasp the concept.

Poki stared at the ground in silence. It would be disrespectful to demean an older person, especially a chief. Jim sat cross-legged on the ground, playing with a stick. Even though his eyes were open, I knew he was praying. An awkward silence followed. Finally, Jim looked straight at the chief.

"Who do you pray to?" he asked.

"I pray to the spirits."

"God tells you not to have any other gods, only Him."

Total silence. Not even a tree leaf stirred.

"Yes," the chief said at last. "It's true. I don't pray to God." Jim had translated the Ten Commandments, and Ledu knew the first one well.

Some discussion followed. The men agreed that because they prayed to ancestor spirits they disobeyed God and were therefore all bad.

As the men talked, I climbed the stairway to visit Ahmara, a balding, frail woman. She sat by the fireplace in the middle of the house. The room was swept clean, and her warm eyes sparkled a welcome when she saw me. She reached above her head to the rafter and pulled out a woven mat.

"Jaki, sit down," she murmured, unfolding the mat for me to sit on. "I'm not afraid to stay by myself when my daughter leaves to work in the garden now," she exclaimed. Her gnarled hands were gentle as she stroked the ashen fire with a stick. "I sit here every day and think about God." I smiled at her trusting face. "And I wait for Sunday to come so I can hear Poki tell more about God."

"Thinking about God is a good thing," I assured her. "Pray to God, and He will take care of you."

Ahmara nodded at me, acting like she understood. Then she began rocking back and forth, singing fragments of the first hymn Vida wrote.

Next I visited Namiji, an older woman who worked hard, and often did things to help other people. She was sitting on the ground with a bunch of puppies, some in her lap, some nuzzling on wobbly legs beside her. She was eating cooked bananas and flashed me a big, banana-filled smile. Namiji chewed the banana to a soupy substance and spit the mixture onto leaves for the puppies to lap up. Astonished I asked, "Why are you doing that?"

"The mother died last night," she explained. "If I don't feed the babies, they'll die." She smiled at me again and put another banana into her mouth. Then she picked up a puppy and forced some banana from her mouth into the puppy's.

I dropped down next to this woman with the heart of gold and picked up two puppies, scratching their ears and petting their fur. Avovo, her four-year-old son, sat on the stairs of the house, whimpering. No one paid any attention to him, and the whimpering grew louder. When his sniveling got on my nerves, I asked the boy, "Why are you crying?" He looked at me, but instead of replying, he threw himself onto the ground and began groveling in the dirt, screaming.

"He wants me to feed him my breast milk," Namiji explained, unperturbed.

"What? He's too old to be breast-fed," I protested. The undisciplined child continued his tantrum, smearing his body with filth as he rolled around on the ground, sobbing. I wanted so badly to get up and spank him.

His mother put the puppies aside patiently and stood to lift the naughty child from the ground and put him to her breast.

Immediately, the crying stopped, and the spoiled child sucked contentedly on the worn-out breast. "He's my last baby, so I'll nurse him for a long time," she said, the kindness never leaving her face. I knew it was their custom not to discipline children, but nursing a four-year-old was ridiculous. I wondered if Avovo would ever amount to anything worthwhile.

The sun climbed directly above us. Namiji moved one arm across her forehead to wipe the perspiration. "Did you hear that our villages will move halfway down the mountain?"

"Yes, we heard. But is it really going to happen?"

"The government patrolman said we had to move."

"Why?"

"He said it's too cold to live on top of the mountain; many of our babies catch cold and die. So we must move down where it's warmer. We'll be together—Numba and Sivurani—one big village."

A bad feeling descended upon me. I did not know if I wanted the villages to be combined or not.

Suddenly, the smile disappeared from Namiji's face. "Mararija's sick," she said of her husband. "He can't build our house in the new village until he gets well."

"What's wrong with Mararija?"

"Whenever he goes to the bathroom, there is blood," she said, and her forehead furrowed in worry.

Oh, no, I thought. *Dysentery! We don't have medicine for that.*

Jim strolled over carrying Rick and joined us. "Whee," he said, mimicking their expression for surprise. "Your baby's too big to drink breast milk." Namiji gave Jim the same happy smile she gave me. Quickly, I explained about Mararija's sickness.

"I'll call on our radio tomorrow morning," Jim said to Namiji. "I'll ask the doctor to send some medicine on Thursday's plane."

Namiji looked relieved.

On the road home I asked Jim, "How will Mararija know when to take his medicine? We won't be here."

"I'll have to tell his son Chululu when to give it to him. If he doesn't give the medicine faithfully, his father will probably die."

With that grim thought we reached home and began packing. We were scheduled on Thursday's flight to Ukarumpa where we would await the birth of our second child.

Randy James, our second son, was born on May 1, 1966. A few weeks later, we moved into our house in the new village of Numba as a family of four.

Friends came daily to help us build our house in the new village. Jim noticed the poles they brought made of good, hard wood. No signs of termites, either. One day as he and Poki banged in a corner post, Jim remarked, "The wood the men brought for our first house was no good. Why didn't they bring strong wood like this?"

Poki laughed. "Nobody wanted to waste their good wood," he said, still laughing. "The Numba people didn't want you to stay, they told us you would be leaving, so we went into the forest and got our worst wood."

Jim's mouth dropped open. "So, your people didn't want us," he said, tongue in cheek, pretending to be offended. "They just gave us rubbish. I guess we should go back to America."

"No, no, no!" Poki quickly replied, waving his hand back and forth in protest. "That was before, not now. Everybody wants you to live with us, now. That's why they all brought the best wood." Poki's face filled with concern. He thought Jim's comment was serious. I looked at my mischief-making husband and shook my head.

Mane'unoma, the oldest warrior still living, had slain many enemies and eaten their flesh. Flaps of skin, no longer filled with the muscles of youth, hung loosely from his arms and thighs as he sat in the doorway of his house holding Randy. As I stood nearby, taking in the scene, the image of the old year going out, and the new coming in, came to mind.

I tried to imagine what he could have looked like as a fierce warrior. I studied his hands—hands that once killed and maimed

Hands that once killed now caressed Randy, our second son.

were now loving as he caressed our son, stroking the silken hair and sniffing Randy's sweet-smelling baby skin. Randy, a placid baby who rarely cried, did not seem to mind the woolly, gray beard scratching his cheek as the old warrior continued to sniff and kiss him.

Jim and I brought back a large supply of medicine for dysentery. In the evenings, we visited Mararija to make sure he took the right dosage. The sick man would push himself up to a sitting position when we arrived so he could talk from a normal position.

"When I get better," he said to Jim, adjusting his blanket around his shoulders, "I want to come to your Bible study on Saturday nights. My son Ajanipa goes; afterwards, he comes back and tells me about God." Mararija's emaciated chest moved up and down at an accelerated rate. Each breath was a struggle. Yet his eyes held hope that one day he would be well. Namiji's wide, gummy smile reflected the same hope as she offered us taro with pumpkin tops to eat.

Two nights later, after we had gone to bed, we heard a moaning sound coming from the village. The sound stopped abruptly, and we drifted off to sleep. Soon afterwards, the wailing began. I woke up to hear village dogs howling along with the high-pitched cries. Above the cries we heard angry shouts. "I'd better see what's going on," Jim said, pushing back the covers.

"I'll go with you," I said, springing out of bed and feeling around on the floor for my rubber thongs.

"You'd better stay in case one of the kids wakes up," Jim said, and, still half asleep, I sank back down into bed.

The wailing continued through the night. *Don't let it be Mararija,* I thought, but an ill-fated feeling came over me, telling me it was he who died.

I listened for the sound of Jim's footsteps on the porch until dawn lightened the sky. The house shook slightly as he came up the stairs and in through the front door. I jumped out of bed and met him in the hall.

"Who died?" I blurted out, then held my breath.

"Mararija died," he replied, and my heart sank.

Oh no, I thought, as the image of Namiji's face came to mind. I ached for her. Numbly, I followed Jim back into the bedroom. He looked exhausted. "Who's doing all the yelling?"

"Chululu," he said, getting under the covers. "Chululu's angry and tearing down everything. First he went to his father's gardens and chopped down every banana and papaya tree. He told people that no one would eat the food his father had planted."

"But wasn't Chululu afraid to go to the garden after dark?"

"He must have been too upset to care. And after he came back, he chopped down the new house that he and his brothers had just built, and flung all their belongings out into the middle of the village. Namiji went to stay in Ajanipa's house. That's where the body is too. The house is full of people."

"The village has lost a good-hearted man," I said, feeling sad that this dear man was gone from our lives.

Pupuri also cried, the young, pretty teen who "gave her heart" to Chululu. The couple waited for Mararija to be well enough to perform the village ritual of marriage. Now it would be up to Ajanipa, the oldest son, to take her hand and place it in his brother's and say the words that would seal their marriage.

Two weeks after Mararija was buried, the wedding took place. Pupuri's father grasped his daughter by the wrist and led her to Isoro's house where the newlyweds would live until their house was build. Ajanipa, almost as frail as his father had been, stood breathing heavily as he waited in front of the house to perform the ceremony. Family members brought newly woven mats, cooking pots, and coins that added up to about $9. It was considered a good bride-price.

The young bride did not wear a new bark cloth nor special beads, but dressed as she would for any other day of the week. She stood to Ajanipa's left and giggled nervously. Chululu walked over with a calculated brusqueness and stood on the other side and stared straight ahead, his face a mask of stone. Pupuri's nose wrinkled up with laughter after her last giggle. Then, when all grew quiet, her lips trembled.

Ajanipa took Pupuri's hand and placed it into Chululu's confident grasp. "Marriage is a good thing to do," he said to the bride and groom. "You must plant good gardens together and have a big family...."

The ceremony was over. Chululu and Pupuri were now man and wife. "I hope he doesn't crush her sweet spirit with his obnoxious ways," I remarked to Jim, afraid for the docile girl.

"Maybe marriage will settle him down," Jim replied. "I hope so. I've asked him to check the translation that Poki and I are working on. He's the best reader in the village."

"What did he say?"

"Nothing. When I mentioned the idea, his mind seemed a thousand miles away. I don't think he heard what I said, but I'll ask him again."

Chululu proved to be an excellent translation checker. Having another person with whom to discuss difficult concepts was helpful. For example, because the Managalasis had never seen snow, the phrase "white as snow" needed an equivalent that would relate to their culture.

"What's very white that has no dark spots in it?" Jim asked.

Chululu and Poki talked a bit, then agreed on a "cockatoo." So, at the bottom of verse three in Matthew 28, it read: "...and his clothes became like (the color of) a cockatoo." Jim checked this out at the next men's study, and everyone seemed to understand.

One Thursday evening, Pupuri, wrapped Indian-style in a new blanket, came to the house so we could walk to the women's Bible study together. I handed her the gas lantern to carry. When we reached the doorway of their house, Chululu bounded out unexpectedly. He struck his wife across the head with the back of his hand. I cringed when I saw the terrible, merciless expression on his face as he yanked the blanket from her shoulders and spun her around before she fell, smashing the glass of the lantern. The arrogant man then covered himself with the blanket and stormed back to the house without a backward glance.

Pupuri sat on the ground, stunned. My heart went out to the young bride, and I rushed to her side to help her up. No sound emerged from her lips, but giant tears lay on her cheeks. "Sorry," she murmured. "Sorry for breaking your lamp."

"Don't worry," I said assuringly, "Jim has another glass at home. He'll fix the lamp."

Others gathered to see what had happened.

"Chululu's a bad man," they were saying.

"He was mad because I took the blanket," Pupuri explained for her husband.

There's no hope for this despicable, cruel man, I thought as anger churned within me. *And his reading the Bible everyday apparently hasn't done a bit of good.*

After Bible study, I waited until my eyes adjusted to the darkness outside and walked home more by instinct than sight. "Aren't you afraid the spirits will bite you?" some of the women asked as I passed by.

"No, God is with me, and I'm not afraid." As I strode towards home, I wondered if these women would ever walk in the dark alone trusting God totally, not fearing evil spirits.

At home, I gave the broken lamp to Jim and told him what had occurred.

"That's too bad," Jim said. "Chululu's so sharp when it comes to finding errors. I was hoping that with his keen mind, reading the Bible everyday, eight hours a day, would help..., but I guess not," he ended sadly.

"I **know** not," I underscored with disgust. "His disposition is rock-hard! Nothing will ever soak through."

For the last two weeks, going home filled my every thought, penetrating even into my sleep. I spent the nights dreaming of my family in Nutley, and the days turning memories over in my mind. I remembered things like Mom and me shopping in the malls, laughing together in front of the TV watching Jackie Gleason or the "I Love Lucy" show, the two of us meeting my sister Mary Lou for lunch, and holidays with the house smelling of lasagna, turkey and chestnuts.

1967 already. Five years had gone by since we left New Jersey. Now we were on our way to the States for a one year furlough. As we boarded the jet in Port Moresby, I wondered how Jim and I would hold up—traveling sixteen hours with two small children. But, as it turned out, I had nothing to fear. Randy, a year and a half, slept most of the time, and Rick, three and a half, busied himself with his "G.I. Joes" and a coloring book. Nary a whimper out of either of them.

Five hours into the trip, I grew restless. Three more hours and my stomach felt like it was knotted up. After an entire night of anxiety, the plane finally arrived at Newark Airport in New Jersey. Stepping onto the moving passageway that led to the airport was like the last stretch for the runner, the final draft for the writer. The hallways of the aiport became crowded highways, and I gulped, wondering how we would connect with my family in this mass of people.

Jim, carrying Randy and a tote bag, took charge. "This way," he said confidently, motioning with his head. I took a deep breath, gripped my purse and tote in one hand and Rick's hand in the other.

Moving through the corridor was arduous. Weary travelers, luggage, airport attendants, and people movers littered the place. My hand throbbed from carrying my tote, and, just when I thought, *I can't hold on to the plastic handle for one more step,* I heard a familiar voice calling, "Jude! Jude!" I looked over and saw my sister Mary Lou jumping up and down, waving jubilantly. My pain forgotten, I nodded vigorously in response. Then I spotted Mom, happy and excited; my brother Bill and his wife, Maureen; and Dad, looking the same as ever wearing his gray Fedora hat.

"There they are, Rick! Over there!" I pulled him through the crowd to the baggage area where we were free to embrace and greet each other. Mom's face beamed as she hugged Rick. "Do you remember Grandma?" she asked the speechless child. "I took care of you when you were a baby." Rick's chin sunk deeper into his chest like a turtle withdrawing into a shell. He looked frightened in this village of jabbering throngs.

All of us talked at once as we waited for our suitcases to appear on the moving belt. "How was your trip?" Billy asked, bending over to pick Rick up. Grandma snuggled Randy, cooing to him.

"The trip was interminably long," I replied, "but the stop in Hawaii helped. When we saw McDonald's, we rushed to buy hamburgers and fries. As soon as I sank my teeth into a Big Mac, I felt like I had come home."

Engulfed by my family, their faces smiling and their love reaching out to me, I knew I could never be happier than this.

At the missions conference in our home church, I prepared to tell how I felt when we landed on the little New Guinea airstrip for the first time. Would these friends in the congregation think me unspiritual if I revealed my true feelings? Dr. Anderson sat in the front row, his eyes fixed expectantly on me. I swallowed, then confessed how I had longed to get back into the plane never to return to those Managalasi people—ever! I held my breath, wondering what their reaction would be. I looked at my pastor first. Was I seeing right? He sat in the pew laughing so hard he had to get out his handkerchief to wipe his eyes. Greatly relieved, I proceeded to tell all with special emphasis on the spiritual warfare. As I concluded, I assured everyone that I had no doubt their prayers had taken me through many difficult situations and kept me from giving up.

Afterwards, friends gathered around promising to uphold us in fervent prayer. Certainly, that was the best thing they could do for us because without prayer we would accomplish nothing.

During the year, we traveled to other states and presented our work many times over. Hauling the boys from church to church or from home to home, week after week turned into a grueling experience. Speaking to women's groups came easily, but afterwards, relating on a one-to-one basis seemed awkward. Even with close friends I found it painful to communicate. While they were here living life as usual, I had changed. Living among the Managalasis, I had evolved into an entirely new person.

It seemed strange to feel so different from these friends with whom I had grown up, these friends with whom I had joked and engaged in pranks; disappointing to feel their disinterest in many aspects of my new life; uncomfortable, for they did not relate to such a lifestyle.

Soon it was time to pack up and return to Papua New Guinea. Our furlough year passed by too quickly. I wasn't ready yet. I didn't shop enough at the mall, nor eat enough of Mom's cooking, nor spend enough time with my brother and sister.

With the car packed nearly to bursting, we drove over to Mom and Dad's house to say good-bye. Parting at the airport would have been too final, too cruel. From their house we planned to drive to Tennessee and say farewell to Jim's folks.

Dad sat in front of the TV wearing his favorite faded, plaid flannel shirt. He was filling the bowl of his pipe when we walked in. "Well, look who's here," he said smiling at his grandsons who headed straight towards him. He moved over in his large leather chair, making room for them. Mom had perked coffee, and we sat together in the kitchen for one last time. Then, the dreaded moment arrived when we would have to part for another five years. Another **long** five years.

Dad and Mom walked out with us to the black Chevrolet parked in front. I wanted to tell them I loved them, but could not speak. I hugged them both and quickly jumped into the car, then occupied myself with arranging the boys in the back seat...a suitcase in between to keep squabbling to a minimum.

"Oh, I forgot something," Mom said and hurried back into the house. She scurried back and handed me a pink and orange-flowered umbrella adorned with a carved shiny wood handle. "I remember all the rain at Ukarumpa, so I bought this for you as a parting gift." With an encouraging smile, she said, "Think of me when you use it."

"I always think about you, Mom," I whispered, brokenly. Jim started the car, and it rolled forward. Mom stood next to Dad in her striped housecoat. She saw my pain and flashed me a brave smile. "Don't worry, Jude, the years will fly by and, before you know it, we'll be together again.'

The two figures standing in front of the brick house became a blur as our car glided down the hill toward Route 46. I sobbed for hours as we drove along. The boys sat quietly in back. Turning to check on them, I saw fear in their eyes, for they had never seen their mother cry before. This blubbering had to stop for their sake. When we stopped in Virginia to have a bite a few hours later, I was still clutching the umbrella with both hands. My parting gift was bright and cheerful, just like Mom. It was difficult to let go.

Section Three

Turning Points

Turning Points

"In twenty minutes we'll be landing in Port Moresby," the pilot announced. Outside my window stretched the rugged, mountainous coastline of Papua New Guinea, bold and brilliant against a blue sky. I felt as excited as a child on Christmas morning. *Why should I be so excited? This isn't my home! Perhaps it's because the long trip is finally over, and soon we'll make our last trip through Customs. Of course, that explains it.*

Waves of heat engulfed us as we stepped off the plane and down the steps. Randy's hand felt sticky in mine as we shuffled toward the terminal. Steam from the ground swept upwards and disappeared beneath the scorching sun.

Jim looked tense as we stood in line with our suitcases. Our luggage held a lot of new articles. "I hope I have enough money to pay the customs' fees," he said.

"We only have two suitcases each; that's what customs allows. Why are you worrying? Do you think we'll be overweight?"

"No doubt about it!"

When it was our turn, Jim flung the suitcases on the counter, and we started to open them.

"You're Jim Parlier, aren't you?" the inspector asked. Jim looked surprised. "Yes," he replied, reaching out to take the extended hand in his.

"Dad and I visited you in Numba Village a few years ago. My father was on a medical patrol, and we left you with some medicine."

"Oh, yes," Jim said quickly with a smile of recognition.

"Don't bother opening those," he said, waving his arm as a signal for us to move on. "Just go on through." Gratefully, we shook hands a second time, and went ahead.

From the terminal, we took a taxi to the Mapang Guest House where we were registered for the night. The SIL plane, scheduled to arrive in the morning, would take us to Numba Village. But first, we had to visit some Managalasi friends who worked at a store called "Beeps." At the guest house, we arranged for a rented car and set out to find them.

The sun poured gloriously through the coconut palms as we drove up in front of "Beeps." Four of our friends, all young Managalasi men, stood outside talking. Chululu's brother, Ometa, spotted us as we drove up. He poked the others. Surprise, then joy splashed across their faces. I wanted to rush over and hug all four of them, but in their culture women didn't do that, so I stood by the car nearly bursting with excitement.

"Jimmy! Jaki!" they yelled over and over, as Jim headed towards them. The four of them rushed to meet him and I joined in. Their arms closed tightly around us, clinging to us, as if we, like steam, would evaporate if they let go. Startled onlookers stopped to watch, forming a large group. So enthralled were we in each other, that none of us cared as they gathered around to gape. Even Jim, who shied away from public affection, looked happy, with no trace of embarrassment on his face.

We pulled up chairs at one of the tables and chattered happily. Ometa brought over four cokes for us to quench our thirst. Then, Ometa and his cousin Kola scooped up Rick and Randy, lifting them high over their heads and onto their shoulders. They galloped around the tables, pretending to be horses carrying two cowboys. They yelled and giggled until exhaustion forced them to quit.

Later that night I asked myself, *Why since these people are not my relatives, do I feel the same elation I felt when greeting my own family? And Rick and Randy...they don't act the least bit shy. The pleasure on ther faces indicates that our sons do not live in two cultures as Jim and I do; only one culture lives in their hearts. As far as the boys are concerned, they have been away on a visit to a foreign country for a year and have finally come home.*

The next day the SIL plane picked us up at the Port Moresby terminal. With the help of a tail wind, we flew over familiar landmarks only thirty-five minutes after take-off. The mountains loomed in sweeping rims, dwarfing Numba Village below. My body tingled when our house, standing like a Swiss chalet to the left of Numba, appeared. The wheels touched down gently on the strip, and we were as good as home.

A throng of excited, smiling faces eagerly awaited our arrival. Again, excitement mounted within me, and I could hardly wait to get out of the plane.

"Esa'ua," I called to a few ladies who waited near the cargo shed. Some of the younger boys ducked in front of me and whisked Rick and Randy away. The crowds started moving in closer with outstretched hands. "The beads on your neck are mine!" a voice yelled. I looked up to see Kanuji, one of the older women.

"No, they're mine!" another voice said.

"Oh, Jaki, give them to me," Kanuji pleaded, moving close and grabbing hold of the hot-pink plastic beads I wore. "Give them to me, I'm your 'mother.'"

All at once the happiness left me. *This lady never claimed me as her daughter before,* I thought. *She just wants my beads.* "'Mother,'" I responded, sarcastically, "I've been away for almost two gardens. Is this how you greet me after not seeing me for many moons?" I felt sad and disappointed.

Our house, like a Swiss chalet, stood near the Numba village.

"Jaki, it's true, I didn't ask how you enjoyed being in America. I'm sorry," Kanuji admitted, still eyeing my beads longingly. Then she added, "But please don't give them to anyone else, give them to me."

I looked for Poki, but could not find him anywhere among the crowd. Jim listened patiently to some of the men. "We didn't have any blankets while you were gone," they complained. "We were too cold to sleep. There was no fish to eat, no meat." Then they asked hopefully, "Did you bring us any soap?...fishhooks?...matches?...kerosene?...cloth?"

No doubt about it, the villagers were glad to have us back. But...was it us they were glad to have back, or the things we could provide for them? Yet I could not blame them for the way they felt. In their eyes, we had so many comforts while they, so few.

A late arrival pushed through the crowd to Jim's side. His hair was matted, like it hadn't been combed in months. Soot and dirt smeared the muscular chest, arms and legs. The unfamiliar figure talked rapidly, then suddenly burst out with laughter. *Where have I heard that laugh before? Only one person convulses into laughter like that. But it couldn't be.* I moved closer to check on the face, now split wide open with a red-toothed smile. Yes, it was really him, but what happened to him? What made him look so different...so terrible? And, Poki never chewed betelnut before.

"Poki's different now," Sonalu confirmed as we walked to the women's Bible study together. "He doesn't teach the old people on Sundays anymore, either."

Before we left on our trip to the States, Sonalu had accepted Christ as her Savior. It felt good to talk to another believer.

"Does he pray to the spirits?" I asked anxiously.

"No," she replied, and hesitated. I relaxed. At least Poki had not gone back to the old ways of worshiping. "But he doesn't think about God like he used to before you left," she added.

Sonalu, God's gift to me, was the first girl to become a Christian.

"Maybe when he starts helping Jim put God's words into your language again, he'll think more about God," I said, hopefully.

"Maybe," Sonalu conceded, but her eyes looked doubtful.

We reached the lower end of the village, and I began calling out the women's names. "Kanoha, come, it's time for our meeting! Topu, come! Vivi, let's go!" Calling them by name was like sending an engraved invitation, and the women rarely turned down the offer.

The room filled up quickly with eager, chattering faces. Once they settled down, I began reviewing the verses we had learned over a year ago. Next, we began prayer time.

"Pray for my back, it hurts from bending over in the garden," Kiji requested. "I've been praying to the spirits, but my back still aches, so ask God to heal me."

Her alarming admission filled me with dismay. "You can't pray to two gods," I rebuked. My tone was a tad sharp, but I was tired of their double-minded ways. These women had listened to God's Word for over five years, had memorized many Scripture verses, and sung hymns praising God every week. When were they going to stop worshiping ancestor spirits and totally trust God?

"Wait for me!" a bold voice ordered from outside.

"Who's that?" Namiji shot back.

The room fell silent. Footsteps on the stairway creaked beneath the weight of the latecomer. All eyes flew to the doorway. "Wait for me," the voice repeated. "I belong to the devil, and here I come!" In pranced Kanoha, Morisi's mother. She pretended to be dancing and hopped in the customary rhythm, shaking invisible shakers and bobbing her head. "When I die, I'm going to the fire," she laughed, and squeezed in next to her sister-in-law, who laughed back at her.

Her brazen outburst left me speechless. Snickers broke out among the women, and I felt my face getting warm, anger welling up inside.

"I belong to the devil, too," another said. "Me, too," agreed another. "Someday we'll all be squirming in the fire like worms squiggling in bamboos when we roast them."

This brought hearty laughter from everybody. Their shameless attitude appalled me, and an ugly feeling invaded the room, making me feel that if I didn't belong to the devil, I wasn't with the "in-group." I felt the full force of Satan's undivided kingdom.

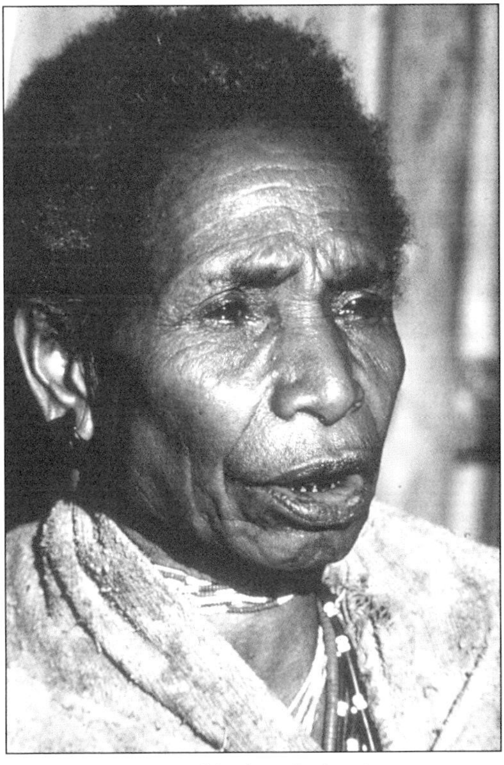

Kiji prayed both to God and to her ancestor spirits to heal her.

In my mind I knew God existed, but at that moment I could not sense His power. I became a spectator in Satan's synagogue. I began to perspire, yet the moisture on my forehead felt cold. I stood up slowly, gaining their attention, and the group started to simmer down.

"You cannot belong to the devil and belong to God at the same time," I told them. The tremor in my voice sobered them.

Chipi, sitting with a sneer on her face, blurted out, "These women don't want God. They hear God's story, but they want the devil's ways; they're all liars." Then she sat back with a defiant look, daring the women to deny her words. No one contradicted her, nor did they remind her that she, too, acted no differently than they.

I tried to reason with them. "If you didn't want God's ways, you wouldn't have come to hear His talk tonight."

Namiji spoke up, "Yes, we want God. We love to hear His talk, and we like to sing the hymns. While we are here with you, we are happy. We think about God. But, when we go home, we forget God and think about the spirits again."

I looked at Sonalu. Yesterday she refused to wash clothes in the river by herself because she was afraid. Two people died during the week before we returned, and in the minds of these people, there were two spirits lurking about, seeking other victims. Sonalu, a Christian, should have known better, but she also believed this direct lie from Satan.

"There are no spirits," I said, but my words fell flat. The women glanced at each other and began to mumble. I sensed it might be useless to teach the lesson I had prepared, and I became the target for Satan's fiery darts of doubt.

"Let's sing again," I suggested, determined to keep Satan from winning this battle.

"Let go of your sins and believe God," the women sang, half-heartedly. As soon as the song ended, I plunged into my lesson. But my words sounded hollow, and the spirit of unity which I normally felt with the women...gone. I ended the lesson lamely, and left the house without staying to chat.

Feeling defeat in my soul, I walked home slowly, wondering if perhaps the "Father of Lies" had won a victory after all.

All week long Sonalu tried to wheedle me into being her partner at the sing-sing. The party signified the end of their planting season—the gardens had been burned off, cleaned, and replanted. It was time to celebrate with an all-night party.

My first response was an adamant "No," but Sonalu continued to follow me around whimpering and pleading.

On the day of the party, as I taught Rick his school lesson, Sonalu popped in with a new bark cloth. She wrapped it around me and said, "When everybody sees you wearing this, they'll be so happy."

I knew it had taken her a week to pound out the bark, dry it, then paint on the designs. I could no longer refuse her. "Okay," I said, "I'll be your partner."

Anticipation stirred in the village as women prepared yams, greens and cooking bananas to be steam-cooked in a pit dug in the ground. Fires already heated large rocks inside the pit. Men sat inside their houses bent over feathers, spending tedious hours positioning each one to lay exactly right on their headdress. Some young children were sent to fetch firewood. Others weeded the entire village and swept it clean. Teenagers tied sugarcane onto long poles for the visitors to take home in the morning.

Necklaces made from shells, coffee seeds, and cassowary bone weighed me down as I walked to Sonalu's house to have my face painted red. "Wheyyy, wheee," the young children exclaimed, seeing me approach the village modeling my red and yellow bark skirt.

Everyone stopped their work to stare. Whisperings of "Jaki's a 'young girl,'" went around the village.

"Here comes an unmarried Managalasi lady," exclaimed Sonalu's mother, obviously pleased with the way I looked. With a wide grin, she placed armbands on both of my upper arms and tucked leaves smelling like anise under each band. She dipped a stick into a thick red mixture and painted stripes on my face and forehead. Lastly, she placed a woven headband around my short, black hair, and I was ready.

As the sun set, the dancers were getting into place, forming two lines. They tapped their kundu drums—made from logs and hollowed out with fire. They stood, tuning their instruments with beeswax on the snakeskin drum heads, adding some or removing some, until all the drums had the same tone. The women stood poised in specified places holding steady their seed pod shakers. The drums began to pound in heavy precision beats, electrifying the air. The women chimed in with their shakers. Chills rippled through my body as I joined in shaking my seed pods. I felt like a true Managalasi woman.

Sonalu and I followed along in line behind Isoro and Chululu, much like doing a square dance or performing the Virginia reel...but without smiling faces. These dancers wore serious, deadpan expressions. I glanced at Sonalu several times. She seemed to frown in concentration. I did not understand it. Why did they look so unhappy? This was a party!

Though my footwork was not as intricate as Sonalu's, I still managed to keep rhythm. Villagers sat along the sidelines with

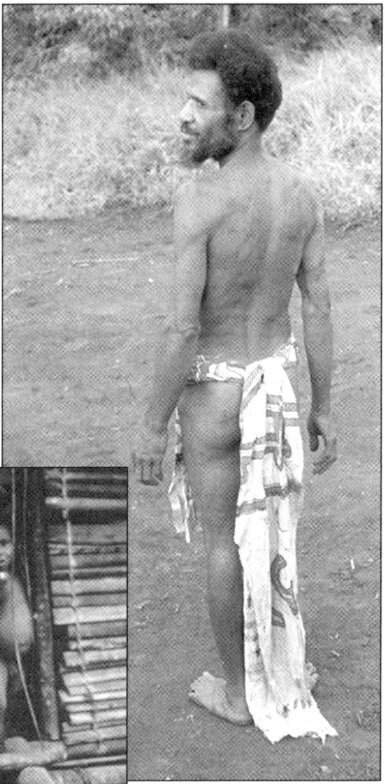

Men wore loin strings made of bark cloth.

Women wore it as wrap-around skirts.

A man's prize possession was his headdress.

Dancers were ready to go home to sleep.

surprised expressions. I heard them utter my name scores of times, and they encouraged me with smiles. I had to admit to having fun. Jim sat alongside them with Randy on his lap. When he saw me for the first time, his eyes bulged and he pretended to go into a state of shock. Later, his broad smile confided to me his pride in see his "Managalasi" wife.

All of a sudden, harsh shouting knifed into the singing and halted the dances abruptly. "Stop!" the voice shouted. Mava, a middle-aged man with an abnormal cloud of white spreading over half his left eye, stood with an angry look. "You're singing badly! Go back to your houses!" he demanded with venom in his tone. "This sing-sing is over!"

Chululu deftly left his place in line and, like a bolt of lightning, knocked Mava to the ground. The teenage girls screamed and ran to their houses. Rumbling and shouting filled the air as several men tried to keep Mava from retaliating. Two men pinned Chululu's arms back, intertwining them with their own. Foul words erupted from Chululu's mouth as he stared Mava down with a stony, determined face.

In a daze, I felt Sonalu's hand on my arm, pulling me back toward her house. I couldn't take my eyes off the many faces. Some extremely angry, others with worried expressions.

Once inside Sonalu's house, we sat by the dead fire while the men carried on with their bickering. Sonalu looked as remorseful as I felt. "Why did Mava stop the dancing?" I asked.

"Mava said our voices didn't sound happy so our singing was no good," she replied, indifferently.

"And so? Should I go home?" I asked.

"No," she said. "They're talking about continuing again. I heard them say that because you, the Big Man's wife, got dressed up to dance, they should finish the sing-sing."

Just then, Sonalu's younger sister, Tootsy, got out of bed and sat beside me.

"If you're too sick to roll cigarettes for Raka, what are you doing out here?" Sonalu demanded.

"I want to sit with Jaki," she replied, trying to rekindle the fire.

"Viiiiii," Sonalu sang on a high-pitched tone that descended the scale to a low pitch. Her black eyes pierced into Tootsy's listless ones. "Go back to bed!" she ordered. When Tootsy didn't move, her sister cursed her. It was the first time I had heard Sonalu swear. Then when she spit on her sister, I got angry.

"God is not pleased with the way you are talking to your sister," I said, keeping my own anger in check.

"She's the younger one. She has to do what I tell her," Sonalu replied.

I lay down on the bare floor and closed my eyes. I was shocked to hear filthy words flow from Sonalu's mouth. I must teach her more about the Christian walk, I concluded, and caught myself dozing off. When I decided to get up and go home to my comfortable bed, Sonalu shook my arm.

"Come on, they're starting to dance again."

Numbly, I followed Sonalu to our position. All the excitement I felt earlier had dwindled away. But just before we started, Mava spoke again. Everyone stood motionless while he talked in loud, demanding tones. I could not understand what he was saying. Then, as if someone had plugged electric power into the crowd, the singing started with zeal. After an hour, Jim strode by with Randy asleep in his arms. "I'm going home," he said, and left with Rick trailing behind, sleepily.

As we continued in the sing-sing, friends came up offering food and drink. With each bite I swallowed and each step I danced, I absorbed more and more of the culture. Never before had I felt more like a Managalasi woman. The party continued all night.

Then the sun began to poke its head over the horizon. "Sonalu, I'm going now," I said, wearily, and hobbled home like a cripple.

Later that morning, I heard Jim and Poki talking in the study, followed by smatterings of sing-sing music, and Mava's voice. I realized that Jim had recorded what Mava said.

I drifted in and out of sleep until Jim came into the bedroom and shook me awake. "Do you know what Mava said last night?" he asked.

Still dazed with sleep, I shook my head from side to side.

"Well, first of all, he stopped the sing-sing because the dancers weren't singing loud enough. The man was afraid that the **spirits** would not be pleased with such weak singing, and that all the food they planted would not grow because of the bad performance."

I sprang like a scalded cat to a sitting position. I was wide awake now. A part of me wanted to hear more, but another part of me was afraid to learn the whole truth.

"Then, just before you started singing and dancing the second time," Jim continued, "Mava prayed to the spirits and asked them to help everybody sing louder and dance better."

"Oh no!" I uttered. "They pray to spirits at parties, too!"

I fell back onto my pillow with the unmistaken realization that the Enemy had infiltrated every part of their lives.

Again the words of my supervisor from years before drifted to mind: "Those people have their own religion. They're happy as they are; why do you want to change them?"

Little did she know that the lives of "those people" were controlled by fear. No freedom to be happy even at a party. *If only I had known then what I just now realized, I would have explained that being constantly afraid is* ***not*** *being happy.*

Yet, I felt bothered by something deeper than my supervisor's words. What was gnawing on my insides? All at once I knew: *The Managalasis danced all night to appease the spirit world... and I took part in it*. I felt numb all over.

Pounding bark from a tree, drying and painting is a week's work.

As I was drying the supper dishes, I heard the boys' laughter on the front porch getting wild. I thought back to the time when we first arrived and the children were afraid of us. When they saw Jim coming with his long machete, they ran to hide. Toddlers would scream until someone "rescued" them. Things were different now. Every day our front porch overflowed with children, joyfully jammed with toddlers and teenagers who lingered from early morning until just before dark. Our house was their second home.

Quickly I put the dishes away and went to see about the laughter. Jim sat cross-legged in front of the fire with several boys, listening to them tell ghost stories. I sat on the bench in back of them and concentrated on Jikaro's words.

"Nobody would walk where Maganaho spit," he was saying, "because everybody was scared that if they stepped on his saliva, something bad would happen to them." Jikaro's cheeks puffed out, chipmunk style, as he spoke. His voice was coarse, and he talked as if he'd had a sore throat all his life. "After Maganaho died, they buried him behind the Mission House so no one would have to walk by his gravesite."

Jikaro talked and the other boys laughed uproariously until the supply of wood disappeared.

"Let's go!" Aparihi said, as the last of the orange-red embers died. The boys stood up promptly, like new recruits obeying a sergeant. Aparihi, one of the older boys, was used to giving orders. "Jim," he said, "light your lamp and take us through the banana trees to the village."

"Why?" Jim challenged, his eyes twinkling. "You boys know the pathway well enough, you don't need a light."

Aparihi didn't see the amusement on Jim's face. "But, Jim," he began to explain, "we've been talking about some of our people who died. We've said their names out loud; that makes them angry."

"Why would saying their names make them angry?"

"It's taboo to say a dead person's name. We shouldn't have, but we did. Now their spirits are waiting behind the banana trees to bite us." Apprehension spread across Aparihi's face. "But your lamp will keep them away," he added, convincingly.

All laughter seemed to have died with the fire. Now the younger boys looked at Jim with fear-filled eyes. Before he could respond, I broke into the conversation.

"Ancestor spirits? There's no such thing," I blurted out, tired of the invisible enemy blinding these people with his lies. The boys looked at me sharply, alarm shadowing their faces.

"How can a spirit bite you?" I continued. "Can you feel his teeth?"

Jikaro couldn't keep quiet any longer. "No," he rasped, pausing to wipe the perspiration from his brow. "We don't feel anything, but after we get home, we may get sick, or even die." The scratchy sound in his voice added to the gravity of the situation.

"And another thing," Aparihi put in, "sometimes the spirit will just climb on your body. It feels heavy, like a huge log on your chest, and it's hard to breathe."

I was incredulous. "Who takes the weight off so you can breathe again?"

"Nobody. But if you lay very still, pray to the spirit and tell him you're sorry, the heaviness will lift and you'll be okay again."

"No way!" I laughed, trying to lighten the atmosphere. "Once a person dies, he can't get up again to bite somebody."

"No, Jaki," all the boys seemed to say at once. A sense of panic filled their voices.

"It's taboo to say the name of a dead person," Jikaro repeated patiently, as if trying to enlighten a second grader. "Something bad can happen to you. Maybe your garden won't grow, or the spirits might make your children get sick and die."

Okay, I thought, *these kids have been blinded by Satan long enough. I'm going to do something about it—now!* I walked to the edge of the porch and faced the banana trees. "Ekileta," I yelled out. Ekileta died long before Jim and I came to live with the Managalasi people, but we heard he was a great warrior, and now a powerful spirit.

"Jaki—stop!" Aparihi pleaded. The boys covered their ears with both hands and huddled closer together. Their display of ungrounded fear urged me on to more daring conversation with other dead people.

"Ekileta, can you hear me?" I called out again. "If you can, come and bite me. I'm waiting for you!"

I turned around to see Aparihi's mouth open and close, but nothing came out. The younger boys lay flat on the floor, their hands, like earmuffs, still covering their ears. For a moment, it was if thunder had clapped at the ceiling of the porch.

Hoping a carefree attitude would break the spell of fear, I laughed again. "See! Nothing's happening to me. Where's the spirit?" I challenged. "Why isn't Ekileta biting me?"

No one moved or said anything. Feeling smug, I faced the trees again and began calling out the names of every dead person I could think of. "Magunaho, Machare, Avami..." When I said "Avami," my village mother's name, they gasped in unison. The older woman possessed magical powers while she lived. I remembered the day I put her stringbag on my head and tried to walk. Several young boys sat and laughed at me. Avami uttered some powerful words that sent them fleeing in fear for their lives. Since her death eight years ago, no one dared mention her name. I glanced at Jikaro who looked absolutely stunned.

"Jaki, don't call any more names," he begged with controlled urgency. One of the younger boys started to cry. Aparihi put his arm around the sobbing boy's shoulder. "Jim," he said, "the small boys are too scared to move, you'll have to take them to their houses." Jim reached for the matches.

"You're believing a lie," I said, standing as firmly as a rooted tree. "When a person dies, his spirit goes either to live with God, or to live with Satan. But no spirits remain on the earth to lurk in trees and wait to bite people."

Without a word, Jim lit the lamp and started for the village. He always respected what the boys told him about spirits and didn't argue with them about it. Instead, he patiently taught them what the Scriptures said, then prayed they would soon believe. But Jim's method was taking too long to suit me.

The group scrambled off the porch and flew after Jim like pieces of iron clinging to a magnet. As I watched them go, I saw their genuine fear and my heart felt heavy.

"Lord," I prayed, "how long will it take before these people know the truth? How can I get them to see? Show me how I can make them understand."

Later, when Jim got into bed he remarked, "Boy, you really scared those boys. The little guy was shaking all over. I finally had to pick him up and carry him."

"Yeah," I admitted. "But I had to do **something** to prove how wrong they are, that there are no spirits."

Jim groaned an inaudible reply and I knew he was half asleep. I lay in bed listening to flying foxes flap their wings outside the bedroom window and thought about how terrified the boys were when I called Avami's name. *There must be some way I can prove to them that ancestor spirits aren't real,* I thought, and turned on my side, ready to call it a day.

A few hours passed when an eerie presence entered the room and awakened me. Suddenly I felt a heaviness on my chest, like the weight of a huge log, pinning my body to the bed. I realized what was happening, and tried to wake Jim, but the weight was squeezing every ounce of breath from my body. I couldn't move or speak.

"Dear Jesus, please help me," I prayed, and God began to communicate to me through my mind. Instantly I knew I had to say the name of Jesus and that His blood cleanses us from all sin.

But there was the problem of air—I couldn't get enough to say anything. The weight was pressing down, crushing me, and in one desperate attempt, I forced out the words, "The blood of Jesus," but it sounded like jibberish—nothing a human would comprehend. Yet Satan and his demons understood the message perfectly. The heavy weight lifted immediately, and at last I could breathe normally again.

Quickly, I sat up and watched two red lights, like butterflies, dancing in the middle of the room. "Go away!" I told them. "In the name of Jesus I command you to go and never come back!" The lights flitted over towards the window, slipped through the holes in the bamboo wall, and danced off into the night.

"Jim!" I said, shaking the sleeping figure next to me.

"Hmm? What!" he mumbled.

"I was just attacked by an evil spirit."

"Yeah, right."

"Yes, I really was. And it was just as the boys described—a heavy weight was on my chest, squashing me to death. I tried to catch my breath but couldn't breathe in or out."

"Um hum."

Jim was too drugged with sleep to listen, so I lay back down and turned the event over in my mind. *Was God testing me, or disciplining me?* I wondered. Nevertheless, I felt His awesome presence with me in the bedroom. *He must have allowed me to experience the attack in order to see the enemy's work more clearly; a warning not to dabble in it again.*

A gentle stream of peace flowed from my head down through my spine. God, through His deliverance, had shown me a way to teach my friends not to fear spirits, but to trust Him.

A few days later, I saw Jikaro and told him how the spirit had climbed on my chest.

"You must be teasing, Jaki," he said. "White people don't have spirits climb on their chests, only human beings do."

"What you told me about the spirits is true," I admitted, ignoring the human being remark. "But I'm not afraid to walk around in the dark by myself. The reason is because God is a spirit, and He's larger than any other spirit.

"That's why I wasn't afraid when the bad spirit was on my chest—I knew God would take care of me. And as soon as I said the name of Jesus, the bad spirit went away."

My experience spread through the village like wildfire. Young and old people came to the house asking if the experience were true. They wanted to hear me tell the story in my own words. By admitting there were spirits, I found I had gained a certain credibility with the villagers.

The more I told the story, the more amazed I became, knowing that God, in His grace, didn't snuff out my life for behaving foolishly. He didn't condemn me for my action. Instead He was using my blunder to bring about good for the Managalasis.

"The spirits are real," I said, "but Jesus Christ and the power of God is stronger than any spirit."

A message of hope gripped their hearts and even the attendance at the men's Saturday night Bible study increased. These men wanted to hear more about the spirit who was bigger and more powerful than the spirits they worshiped.

Chululu was the best literacy teacher, even though he was like a grenade with the pin already pulled. Amazingly, he exercised patience with slow learners, and, using analogies from everyday life, gave them easy-to-remember mental pictures to help them learn faster.

After teaching classes, Chululu read over the translation Jim and Poki were doing, checking for errors. Often, he found better ways to express the language. "This is an 'old' word," he would point out. "Only old people will understand this. Let's say it this way...."

One day he checked Revelation 3:20, "...I am standing at the doorway knocking. Whoever hears and opens the door, I'll go inside and live with him and have food with him."

Chululu tapped Jim on the shoulder to get his attention. "Jim," he said, interrupting him and Poki. "What does this verse mean?"

Jim read the verse in question. "'Jesus knocking' means that Jesus wants to come into your heart," he explained.

"Oh," the checker said, taking the book back and reading on. No more was said about the verse, and as usual, when the day ended, Chululu's thoughts about God ended as well. His main concern these days was for his brother, Ajanipa, whose weak heart was getting weaker. The sick man inched his way to the garden every day and sat in the shade, panting for breath, while his wives did the garden work. Yet, without fail, he attended the men's Bible study every week. One night Ajanipa learned that

God could take away his fear of death—an evil force that had tormented him most of his thirty-six years. He wanted to become a Christian but did not think he was eligible because he had two wives. He loved them both; he wouldn't think of leaving one. If he left one of them, then who would provide for her?

He listened carefully to the things Jim taught, and in his heart he believed, but told no one.

One afternoon Chululu sat reading the Scriptures for about an hour without interrupting the translators. Then, he tapped Jim on the shoulder.

Jim, expecting Chululu to point out a problem, turned and instantly noticed something was different about his helper—an unexplainable joy was shining from Chululu's eyes.

"Jim," Chululu said, "For many gardens you have explained God's words to me, but I never let them sink into my heart. Today, as I read His words in my language, it seems like God is talking directly to me. Now I understand what you've been trying to teach me, and I want to become God's child."

Poki and Jim bowed their heads as Chululu prayed and asked forgiveness, then invited Jesus to come into his heart.

Before Chululu left the house, he told Jim, "For many moons and gardens, my eyes were closed, but today God opened my eyes, and I can see."

Early one morning, just before the roosters began to crow, we heard wailing. "Ajanipa must have died," Jim said, and we got out of bed to go to the village. Then, as suddenly as the wailing started, it stopped.

"Shall we go to the village or back to bed?" I asked Jim as he pumped the gas lantern.

"Let's wait a few minutes. If someone starts to wail again, we'll go."

Ajanipa had two wives, but no one doubted he was a Christian.

As we waited, I leafed through a magazine, while Jim scraped under his fingernails with a knife. In five or ten minutes, we heard a knock on the door. Chululu stood there holding a kerosene lantern.

"Ajanipa woke up with strong pain in his chest," he told us. "He couldn't move his left arm. His older wife called for the shaman, but Ajanipa told her no, he didn't want the shaman.

"Then Ajanipa's heart stopped," he continued. "We thought he was dead, but he wasn't—he was praying to God. Later, he sat up. He wants you to come and pray for him, now."

Jim grabbed the lamp and we followed Chululu through the banana trees to Ajanipa's house. The veranda was packed with people.

As we stepped into the house, the crowd shaded their eyes from the blaze of the gas lamp. Ajanipa was sitting up on his mat, happiness and joy written all over his face. "I prayed to God, and He gave me new strength," he announced.

"Tell Jim what you prayed," Chululu coaxed.

Ajanipa looked at Jim with uncertainty, then replied, "I prayed, 'Dear God, if I die, that's OK. I'll go and be with You. But God, my children are small, and I haven't taught them about You yet, so please give me strength to get up again.' He heard my prayer, and I felt God's strength come into my body.

"I told the spirit medium to go away. His ways are the ways of Satan and the fire. I told him to never come into my house again!"

Then, Ajanipa looked steadily into the faces of a disbelieving crowd. "I've been listening to God's Word every week and I believe it," he told them. "Never bring a spirit medium near me again!"

Those who had gathered were stunned by his words. To be on the threshold of death and refuse the spirits' help was unheard of. Word spread throughout the surrounding villages, poking a hole in their world of dark spirits. During the following weeks, attendance at Bible study picked up. Men from other Managalasi villages traveled on foot in the darkness to hear about God's power. "Jim, send someone to our village who can teach us," they begged.

Ajanipa grew stronger and stronger. He kept both wives, yet no one denied he was a Christian.

"It's a girl!" the doctor in Lae Hospital announced, and I closed my eyes, allowing the happiness to tingle all through my body, as though I were bathed in honey-thick sunshine. Jim, who was allowed to stay during the delivery, squeezed my hand

and held it tightly. After eleven years of marriage, he finally had the daughter he'd hoped for. His face glowed.

As the nurse rolled my bed into the hospital room, I thought back to the day we left the village. "Bring back a girl!" the Managalasi women demanded. "Then you'll have someone to help you with your garden." My dry lips cracked into a smile at the memory. The village people called our pantry the "garden," because that was our storage for food. How happy they would be to see Tanya.

Parcels galore came from Mom and Dad. Milky Way candy bars arrived first class airmail. When I protested about the postage, Mom wrote back, "Nothing's too good for my New Guinea kids." But I knew she wanted to be certain we never ate chocolate with worms in it again.

Rick and Randy, hunting and fishing with their village friends, had become fluent in the Managalasi tongue. They knew the names of every tree in the jungle and of every kind of bird that chirped in those trees. Older people would hear them speak Managalasi and beam with pride. Then they would look at me and shake their heads: "Rick and Randy speak our language like true Managalasis, but you and Jim will never speak as well as they do."

One day Randy and his best friend, Jimi, found twigs as sharp as pins and went underneath the village houses. They pushed the twigs through cracks in the floor and stuck the people who were napping. The victims, thinking a spirit was biting, jumped up in alarm and cried out for help. The two rascals under the house would giggle and run off to look for new victims.

"Bring back a baby girl," the women commanded.

Tanya reads her storybook to Chief Ledu.

Rick and Randy learned to trap birds, to fish and speak the language fluently.

All set to go on a family picnic.

Complaints from the village filtered to our ears and we grounded Randy. He had to remain in his room all day. When our friends in the village heard about it, they got upset. Several marched to our house in protest.

"You shouldn't punish your children," Chief Ledu commanded, speaking for the group who came with him. The women looked at me accusingly. "When they grow up," Ledu continued, "they won't take care of you. They won't feed you when you're sick. You'll die hungry."

Jim discusses Bible truths with the men.

My first impulse was to laugh at such a notion, but the serious looks planted firmly on their faces stifled the urge. Jim spoke up, "If our children don't take care of us when we're old, God will."

The hardness visible in their eyes told me they heard Jim's words with their ears, but not their hearts, and there remained the hint of disdain at the corners of their mouths.

Jim launched into a mini-sermon about "sparing the rod and spoiling the child." The women stood listening for a while, then left, but the men sat down on the front lawn discussing the things Jim tried to teach about raising children.

I was about to go back into the house when I saw Rick coming up from the river carrying a string of fish. He looked excited and came running when he saw me. "Mom! Mom! I brought a present for you!"

What could he possibly have brought me from the river? And, especially for a present, I wondered, scratching my head. I waited by the porch, and he proudly handed me his gift wrapped up in large leaves and tied with vine. *A real present!*

How sweet of him to think of me when he's out having fun with his friends, I thought, unwrapping it. Then, when I saw the huge, hairy spider—the biggest I had ever seen—still wiggling, I screamed, dropping *the gift.*

Rick quickly picked it up and took it onto the porch where a few of the boys were already making a fire. They roasted the spider along with the fish, birds and rats they caught in the river and in the jungle. The pungent odor of burning fur drew Randy out of his room to join them. *Not only will we never speak the language like Rick and Randy, but we'll never learn to eat the things they eat either,* I thought, and shuddered.

After dinner I gave out the presents from Grandma and Grandpa—new shirts and shorts for the boys, dolls and cute outfits for Tanya, candy and Halloween masks. Randy's mask was that of a friendly tiger, but Rick's was the face of a fierce Indian warrior. He tied it on and looked in the mirror. He looked pretty frightening, all right.

"I'm going to the village to play a trick on Taiva," he told us. Taiva, now married, read his Gospel of Mark every day and attended Bible study when it was convenient. Still, he feared the spirits and remained an unbeliever.

"You'd better be careful!" Jim warned as Rick traipsed up the path toward the top of the village to Taiva's house.

It was dusk, and Rick moved through the village unnoticed. Most people were in their houses, making fires and cooking. A few of his friends recognized his striped shirt and followed him to Taiva's house. Rick motioned for them to be quiet, and they waited at a distance, watching.

First, Rick peeped through a crack in the wall and spotted Taiva bent over the fire trying to keep warm. His wife, Wasapi, scraped the outside of the yam she was roasting and put it back onto the fire to cook a little longer. Slowly Rick crept up the steps so Taiva wouldn't hear. As he opened the door a tiny bit, it creaked, immediately drawing Taiva's attention. "Yaiy!" he screamed with horror on his face. Wasapi turned around, and she, too, saw the "evil spirit" and screamed wildly. Rick caught sight of Taiva reaching up to the rafters for his pig spear.

In a second, Rick leaped to the ground, running for his life. Isoro lived next door and heard the screams. He had jumped down from his house in time to see Taiva come out with his spear, poised and ready to throw.

"Stop! Stop! It's Ricky, it's Ricky!" the young boys shouted, fearing for the life of their friend. But Taiva seemed deaf to their cries and flung the weapon at the fleeing figure. The spear landed several feet short of its target.

Isoro shook Taiva's arm. "That was Ricky, the 'Long Man's' son." Taiva's face looked gray, and his hands shook nervously. A crowd gathered. "What happened? What happened?" they asked, and the younger boys proceeded to tell the story. Meantime, Rick rounded the back of the houses and appeared, mask in hand, in front of Taiva's house once more.

"Rick, was that you peeking through the doorway?" Taiva asked, his voice, weak. Rick put the mask on again, and all the women screamed. "I heard the door squeak and saw the scary face. I thought it was an evil spirit. Don't do that again," he corrected gently.

"You weren't the only one who was scared," Rick admitted. "I saw you get your spear, and I thought you were going to spear me like you spear pigs."

Laughter erupted from the villagers, and they moved closer to examine the mask. They had never seen such a thing before. The women were afraid to touch it.

Finally Taiva smiled meekly. "Yeah, I almost killed you, my little friend," he said. The smile disappeared from his face as he thought about the consequences.

"I'm sorry, Older Brother," Rick said, and he and Taiva shook hands. "I won't do that again."

"Come," Taiva said, pulling Rick up the stairs by the hand. "Come and eat yams with us."

"Yes," Wasapi called from where she sat. "Come inside and eat, but leave that evil spirit outside!"

I can't recall the exact words written in my sister Mary Lou's letter. I simply remember the nausea, then the pain clutching my insides. "Mom has inoperable cancer."

She can't be dying, I thought. *She hasn't seen Tanya yet.* Without Mom there would be no reason to accomplish anything more in life, no reason to wait for the plane to bring her letters. Now, each time a letter from Mary Lou arrived, the same nausea and intestinal pain would attack my body. The news was never encouraging.

Having my friend, Pat Wiggers, visit us helped keep my mind off the worst thoughts. Pat came to spend several weeks while her husband Ken was at the JAARS Center in Waxhaw, South Carolina.

In addition to providing companionship for me, Pat gave Randy his school lessons every morning, freeing me to do language work. Her humorous comments made me laugh and seemed to numb the sense of impending loss that tormented me from morning till night. My friend, who sensed when I needed her input, yet knew when to listen, was sent to me at that time by God.

On Monday, at 7:00 AM, we listened to the usual radio schedule. The radio operator at Ukarumpa called our code name: "Sierra Oscar," he said, "A telegram arrived for you on Friday. Please stand by."

The word *telegram* sent cold, steel-like claws of pain tearing at my stomach. Would this be the time my long-feared nightmare became real? Instantly, Jim was by my side. "Just prepare yourself," he cautioned in a gentle tone. Then came the message: "Mom died peacefully in her sleep...."

At first I wouldn't allow the news to penetrate, and sensed no pain. Later that day, I taught my women's literacy class as usual. After class I went into the kitchen to bake bread. While the bread was in the oven, I prepared my Thursday night Bible study. Once I heard sobs coming from Jim's office and peeked in the study to see him wiping away tears. Later when the mail came, there was a letter from Mom, just like always.

"Honey," the letter said, "I'm trying out a new recipe for chicken soup. It's got whole tomatoes, cheese...." Suddenly I was back in New Jersey, sitting at the kitchen table watching

Mom stir that soup. It struck me how my vivacious, fun-loving mother lived an ordinary life, doing ordinary things.

We never made important decisions together, solved problems, or resolved major conflicts. We just talked about everyday life, and, as if wired together, burst into spontaneous laughter that left us gasping for breath. Could it be true my best friend was gone? Would I never again see the enormous love for me so evident on her face? Or hear her enthusiastic greeting hastening me into the house when I visited?

I stepped outside into the bright sunlight, but inside, my soul was as black as the caves where bats hung. *Strange that the sun can still shine so brightly and the grass be so vividly green now that Mom is dead. Doesn't the earth have any respect for the death of a great lady?*

I headed toward the village and the final words in the telegram swirled through my mind. "God spared her from a lot of pain and suffering." *He did? How could anybody know that? And what about my deep pain? I would have liked to say good-bye, to tell her how much I loved her, and how hard it would be to wait till I got to heaven to see her again.*

Anger began to build inside. I got mad at God. Very mad. It would have been easy for Him to get rid of the cancer and spare her life.

When I reached the village, only a few people were milling about. Most were working in their gardens. But Tiapa, an elderly man, sat on the grass in front of his house twisting fibers from the banana tree on his thigh. He was making string.

"Jaki!" he called, and I strolled over and sat on the grass beside him. "A lot of us are coming to your house tonight," he said.

"Huh?" I replied, astonished. "Why? What's going on at our house?"

"We want to help you. Your mother died and we're coming to wail with you."

"But she's not your relative," I said, feeling even more astonished. "Why would you cry for someone who's not related to you?"

Without hesitation he replied, "You're our relative, and your heart is filled with grief. You won't be able to cry enough to get rid of that grief by yourself, so we're coming to help you."

I looked at Tiapa with new eyes. *He knows how I feel! This uneducated, caring man understands my pain.* There were no awkward silences in his conversation; he got right to the point and offered the only solution he knew.

For the first time, I felt tears forming and quickly looked away. *Close relatives couldn't be here to share my grief, but God is providing family for me to mourn with.* I could not speak. I felt Tiapa's hand on my shoulder. Somehow he must have seen those tears, felt the lump in my throat. "We'll take turns crying," he said in a soothing tone. "Your grief will finish faster that way."

Unable to meet his gaze, I stood to leave. "It's getting late," I stammered. "The sun is starting to go down. I better go now."

"Good-bye, Jaki. I'll see you later," he said. The kindness in his voice caused burning tears to surface. The path blurred before me. *Tiapa wants to help,* I thought, *but do I really want these friends to mourn for Mom like they mourn their dead—without hope? Death means only hopelessness and darkness to them.*

I hurried up the front steps and realized I didn't want to see my husband, nor Pat, nor anyone, so I continued through the front door and straight out the back. "Lord," I said, "it hurts a lot. I need your peace so badly right now."

As I descended the back steps, the huge sun lodged on the horizon stopped me dead in my tracks. Low clouds cast a dark shadow over the mountains, and they looked as black as death, but the brilliant sky above blazed with light from the orange sun, blending reds and oranges, yellows and purples. It seemed like God himself was pointing out to me that after the darkness of death comes light—His glorious gift of eternal life. Mom was okay. She was with Him. Suddenly I felt peace surging inside me.

"Keep your eyes on the light, not the darkness," a voice inside whispered, and I knew then what I would share with Tiapa and my friends when they came later. *I will tell them about the light God gives His children after death. There will be no wailing for Mom. There will be no loud weeping or moaning to appease her spirit, and I will do my best to explain why.*

Yes, I would grieve. But more than grieving, I would use my loss to poke another hole in the darkness of their world.

It was time for the wet season to begin, but two months passed and still no rain. The ground in the gardens hardened like cement. Carefully planted yams shrivelled under the punishing sun.

Sometimes dark clouds loomed over the village, but they were only teasing. Soon they'd give way to a fiery sun and starch-white clouds would laze along beneath a turquoise sky.

The village people called on Lotuli to perform his ritual and bring on the rain. They prayed to ancestor spirits, begging for help. Teenage boys were sent to place magical stones and plant red flowers in strategic spots throughout the gardens, but nothing was working.

Day after day, I walked around the village and stared at the dogs sprawled flat in the shade beneath the houses as if they were dead. The spring where the Managalasis fetched water slowed to a dribble. The entire land cried out for water, and with each day anxiety climbed with the thermometer.

It was 7:30 PM, time for the women's Bible study. I lit my lantern and stepped out onto the veranda. The sky was a fairy-land of stars exposing the narrow path that led from our house to the village. *Doesn't look like rain tomorrow either,* I noticed sadly. *What will our people do?*

When I reached the village, the smell of wood smoke filled my nostrils. I strolled to the house where we were having the study. Some of the women were already there, chewing betelnut and discussing the pressing rain problem.

"Jaki, ese!" they greeted when my face appeared in the door-way. The hostess reached for a woven mat tucked behind a rafter. She spread the mat flat and patted a spot in the middle.

"Here, Jaki," she offered, "Sit down here." Her warm smile revealed two rows of blood-red teeth stained from chewing betelnut.

"Esa'ua, Ladies!" I replied, returning their smiles. Before sit-ting down I shook hands with everyone, studying each face. They were tired, worn-out faces. Perspiration from earlier in the day had formed roadways on soot-smeared foreheads and cheeks.

"How are you?" I asked each lady in turn.

"No rain," they replied, as though that were the standard answer.

"Jaki, we're all going to be hungry." Kiji's voice rasped from smoking her bamboo pipe for 67 years. Kiji, skinny as a bam-boo pole, worked as hard as five women. Her zest for life

"Without yams to eat, we'll die," Namiji said.

attracted me to her, and the ready smile was always there for me. Now heavy-laden, mournful eyes fastened themselves to mine. "When the harvest season comes, there won't be any yams to reap," she finished, and lay back, numb-like against the wall.

"That's right," Namiji added. She sat next to Kiji, her life-long friend. Namiji popped a betelnut between purple teeth and cracked down on the outer shell. "Without yams to eat, we'll die." Worry-lines etched the corners of her eyes.

"Let's talk to God about it," I suggested, plopping down on the mat. Folding my legs beneath me, I opened my Bible to

1 Peter 5:7 and read: "Cast all your anxiety on him because he cares for you." Jim and Poki had translated the verse, and Vida, using the pattern for mourning songs, had put the words to music. Sonalu began singing the words in the usual high-pitched falsetto. The rest joined in, singing with heart and soul in each word. Their voices filled the room and wafted out into the village announcing that the women's Bible study had begun. When we finished singing, the room was packed. It seemed like every woman in the village had crammed in tonight.

I took out my pad and pen, signaling time for prayer. "Jaki!" Namiji called out from the back corner. "Pray for rain. If it doesn't rain tonight, our gardens will be completely destroyed. We'll all starve."

"That's right!" another said emphatically. The rest of the women nodded, saying, "That's true, Jaki!" They sounded like a giant choir rising in a crescendo. "Ask God to make it rain tonight! If you don't, many will get sick. Some of us will die."

Their insistence sent a flush of panic through my chest. In my mind I could see the myriads of stars sparkling like diamonds across the heavens just a while earlier. No way was it going to rain. Stunned by the boldness of their request, I looked around the room at each person. These women who prayed to ancestor spirits were now willing to trust God as though He were their only hope. Their eyes bore into mine as they waited desperately for my reply.

Frantically, I sent an SOS to God: *Lord,* I prayed, *what on earth should I tell these women?* For an answer, peace welled up within as a verse leaped to mind: "And whatsoever ye shall ask, I will do it." I knew God was putting His promise into my thoughts and wanting me to trust Him now.

"Okay," I said, clearing my throat. I saw relief spread over their faces, as if I had removed a heavy stringbag from their heads.

"Let's pray," I announced and the room fell silent. "Lord, bless Namiji and cause her gardens to grow well," I began, getting right to the point. "Give them an abundance of food this season, so no one will go hungry." I prayed the same for each woman in the room, peeking every once in a while to be sure I didn't miss anyone. Towards the end of my prayer I pleaded. "And Lord, send the rain...tonight!"

After I finished, the ladies settled back and looked satisfied. I unfolded my notes and began to teach from 2 Corinthians 5:17: "If any man belongs to God he is a new man. He stops walking on the old road and walks on the new road." I talked about how becoming a "new man" involved praying to God only, not ancestor spirits.

After twenty minutes, the sound of light raindrops on the sun-worn roof reached my ears. At first, it sounded like many people whispering; but soon grew louder. *Am I hearing right?* I wondered. *No! Impossible!*

As I continued the study, I saw elbows nudge their neighbor. Voices from outside shouted: "It's raining, it's raining!" Suddenly the room filled with feverish activity, like an anthill that's been stirred with a stick. The rain spattered in through the windows. It dripped through openings in the old, weather-faded house. Excitement swept through the room in a wild frenzy. Some of the women hugged each other. I searched for Kiji. She sat leaning lifelessly against the wall, not saying anything. Her tears, mixed with soot and perspiration, formed a dark liquid in the deep pockets below her eyes.

Someone knocked on the wall. Morisi, who often taunted the women about believing in a white man's God, stood outside. "It's raining," he announced, as if we didn't know.

"Yes!" Namiji responded. She was adamant. "And it wasn't the magical, purple plants you laid around your gardens, either. It's God who is making the rain fall!"

"Nor was it Lotuli!" another declared. I listened to them rebuke Morisi and then I tried to bring them back to the Word. "Let's finish our study!" I yelled out, but my voice disappeared in the craziness of excitement. Everyone talked at the same time. There was no question in anyone's mind that it was God who sent the rain.

Why am I so surprised? Even after seeing the rain, why am I finding it hard to believe God answered my prayer?

The room blurred as I slipped deep into thought. *It's my lack of faith. When I prayed, I really didn't believe God would send the rain. These unbelieving women showed more faith in God than I did. Yet God used me, unworthy me. Why would God use an unworthy vessel like me to show His power?*

As I pondered this, I realized that even though I doubted, in His eyes I was still okay. Humbly, I understood a small part of the depth of His love for me.

"Jaki! Jaki!" Namiji was shaking my arm. "Don't teach us any more tonight. Just talk to your God again for us. Tell Him that all of us say 'thank you' for helping us."

I bowed my head again with my women friends who had exercised more faith in God that night than I had. I thanked Him on behalf of everyone, unaware that sending the rain and healing Ajanipa would be the miracles that would turn the Managalasi people from darkness to light.

Section Four

Walking in the Light

Walking in the Light

As I watched Sonalu kneading bread at the kitchen counter, I felt a sadness because she had never married. She'd had plenty of opportunities. Large bride-prices were offered because she worked for us, but she loved only one man, and that man was Olempoka—Poki. I thought back years to the Sunday morning after the service when she motioned for me to come. "Give Poki this food I cooked for him," she uttered in hushed tones, looking around lest someone overhear. "Tell him 'Soso' made it for him, but make sure no one else finds out."

Oh, oh, I thought. *This is it. When a Managalasi girl gives food to an unmarried boy, it's as good as a proposal. Any kind of exchange marks the two involved as engaged.* I knew if her mother found out, Sonalu would be beaten. *But they can't keep this a secret forever. Someone will find out soon.*

Matajasi, Sonalu's best friend, was getting heavier, and the blouses she wore barely buttoned down the back. Talk went around the village about her being pregnant, but the bulging girl denied all rumors. The older boys jeered and made filthy remarks; the younger children ran up to Matajasi and yelled "Dog!" then ran away and giggled. Sonalu's heart ached for her friend who had not confided in her.

"Who could the husband be?" Sonalu asked me one day.

"I have no idea," I answered, truthfully. "Why don't you ask Matajasi? If she's really your friend, she'll tell you."

As we walked through the village later on, we heard one of the boys ask the pregnant girl, "Hey, Dog, who did you sleep with?" The rise of laughter that followed filled Matajasi with loathing. The distraught girl glared back at the boys, her eyes like two ice chips. "Ask Olempoka!" she blurted out. "He's the father!"

When she turned, she saw Sonalu and me standing close-by, and her lips tightened so that a whiteness formed under them.

Sonalu's eyes locked with her friend's. "Is that true?" she asked, the answer she feared written all over her face. When her friend did not speak, Sonalu swung her eyes away, too shocked to feel the pain. A week later, Poki was forced to marry Matajasi, and all hope for Sonalu disappeared like a soap bubble popping into thin air.

Now, three years later, Poki and Matajasi had two children. Coming to the house was still difficult for Sonalu since Poki worked in the study every day. Today he and Jim were translating the last chapter of Revelation.

As Sonalu and I shaped dough into loaves, a knock came at the door. An old woman stood there, one I'd never seen before. Her face looked tired and worn. Half her hair was gone, and the stringbag she carried all her life had carved permanent indentations into her balding head.

"Come in!" I invited. "Come in and sit down." Wordlessly, the stranger followed me inside.

Sonalu stood at the counter, her face and cheeks powdered with flour. She squinted at the stranger. Then her mouth fell open with recognition. "She's from a village on the other side of the mountains," she declared with a welcoming smile.

The two talked a few minutes in the woman's dialect, then Sonalu relayed the news. "This woman walked by herself for two days over steep mountains to come here. She spent the night with relatives along the way."

"Why?" I asked. The woman smiled. Most of her teeth were gone. Her left eye had developed a grayish cloud.

"Her son is sick," Sonalu explained, as the woman stared steadily at me with her good eye. "She wants you to pray and ask God to make him well."

"She walked for two days just for that?" I was amazed.

"Her son is dying," Sonalu said, emphasizing the word "dying." "She heard about how God sent the rain, and how He healed Ajanipa. She doesn't want her son to die, so she came."

The simplicity of the woman's logic reminded me of the woman in the Bible who wanted to touch the hem of Jesus' garment, believing the mere touch would bring healing to her body. This old woman who had never heard one verse of Scripture had the same faith to believe that God could heal her son.

"Of course we'll pray for your son," I said, reassuringly, and her body relaxed. "Sonalu and I will pray right now."

After we finished, Sonalu made hot cups of Milo for all of us which we enjoyed with fresh-out-of-the-oven bread.

"Come and stay at our house tonight," Sonalu offered. Before the woman left, she stood in the doorway and said, "The people of my village want someone to come and teach us about God. All the Numba people are learning to pray to God, but we have no one to teach us. Can you send someone?"

Later, as I cleaned the kitchen, I heard Jim say to Poki, "We're finished!" The sound of their chairs dragging the floor lured me into the study. Poki and Jim were shaking hands. "Thank you for putting up with me all these years," Jim was saying. "Thank you for not leaving the work until the entire New Testament was completed."

Poki hung onto Jim's hand and made a whooshing sound with his mouth. His left hand went to his mouth and he bit down on his forefinger. Sobs choked out from his mouth and his chest heaved, as he cried. Soon the men were hugging each other, and I saw tears streaming down Jim's face as well.

A milestone had been reached, one they worked twelve years to achieve—the first draft of the New Testament. To God be the glory.

Jim, Chululu and Poki formed a committee of six older men to come to our house each evening to check the translation. Poki would read a passage, then ask the men if the meaning was clear. One evening a stranger, about 35 years old, came in with the men. He walked up to Jim and me with his hand outstretched. "When I was very sick, my mother walked over the mountains," he exclaimed with a smile. "I'm the one you prayed for."

"The sun was a third of the way in the sky before setting (about 4:00 PM) when you prayed. That was the exact time I got better. Many people saw me get up, take my towel and go wash. They will tell you it was at the time you prayed. I just came to Numba to say, 'Thank you for praying for me.'"

Jim and I joyfully shook his hand while Poki explained to the committee what had happened. They invited the young man to stay for the checking session. Afterwards, we ate popcorn and talked about the miracles God was doing in Numba Village.

"How did you translate a 'roaring lion' into Managalasi?" the checker at Ukarumpa asked Jim as he checked the Managalasi translation.

"Poki and I substituted 'wild pig,' for 'roaring lion,'" Jim replied. "A wild pig has the same ferociousness to the Managalasis as a lion does for us and if cornered, the pig will attack and devour."

Poki, Matajasi and their family.

Even though Jim had checked through the entire translation with the committee in the village, additional sessions were held at Ukarumpa with an official translation checker, a non-speaker of the village language. His job included examining problem areas to make sure the translation was accurate before the New Testament was printed.

One afternoon our friend Karl Franklin, director of the Papua New Guinea Branch, stopped by for a visit.

"Did you know, Jim and Jaki, that twelve teams finished their New Testaments this year? Our printshop won't be able to handle all that work. It would be good if you could have the Managalasi New Testament printed in the States while you're on furlough."

Accepting the challenge, we boarded the 707 jet and watched the Papua New Guinea mountains slip away. Within minutes we cruised above the South Pacific waters. Rick and Randy sat happily occupied with puzzle books. Tanya slept on my lap. "What printer in America would ever accept such a large undertaking as a New Testament?" I asked Jim.

"Size is not the only problem," he pointed out, pulling a magazine from the seat pocket in front of him. "It's going to take at least $5,000 for printing costs. Then there's the additional cost for shipping from the U.S. to Hong Kong where the books will be bound, plus more money for the covers, and the shipment of books back to Papua New Guinea. How will we raise that much capital?"

I sighed a long sigh and pushed my seat back as far as it would go. I had no answers, and right now I didn't want to think about any. My eyelids closed and I dozed until the meals were served.

Visiting Dad in New Jersey was difficult. The atmosphere of my childhood home had been transformed from one of festivity and warmth to cold emptiness. The walls needed painting and the drapes needed cleaning. How I longed for the sound of Mom's laughter and the aroma of perking coffee and her delicious home cooking. Visiting now, the walls echoed a sad lonely tune, and my heart, like the house, had turned into an aching ruin.

One evening our phone rang. "Hello, Jim?" It was an old acquaintance. "I've got a problem," he said. "Our pastor is away on vacation and the substitute speaker is ill. Would you speak on Sunday morning for us?"

The next Sunday morning, Jim presented the printing need to a large audience in Nanuet, New York. After the service, a young fellow approached Jim with a happy, expectant look. "You know," he said, "it's not by accident I'm here this morning."

Sensing his excitement, Jim shook his hand in welcome and waited to hear more.

"I left New Jersey early this morning for my home in Chicago. As I drove, I wondered where to attend church. In my heart I felt I should stop and attend this church. Now I know why. There is a printer who lives next door to me who would be happy to print your New Testament."

Contacting the printer in Chicago, we found the young fellow true to his word. The printer, Mr. Alonzo Kallemeyn, was happy to accept the large undertaking.

As we spoke to churches, camps, and to various groups across the States, many individuals contributed happily, knowing their money would be used to give the Managalasi people God's Word in their own language. A year later, just before our return to Papua New Guinea, every cent was provided.

While we were in the States raising money for printing costs, interest in learning to read spread thoughout the Managalasi villages. After we returned, people came from other villages, begging to be taught. Jim and I realized we would have to devote the bulk of our time these next five years to a literacy program, one that would extend to all the Managalasi villages on both sides of the mountains.

About a mile away from Numba, the Anglican Mission had set up an elementary school and they taught English to students through grade six. Children from every Managalasi village attended. The headmaster thought it was a good idea for the children to learn to read their own language before learning to read English. Chululu had already begun to teach classes there. This meant that we would not have to travel far to reach every dialect in the Managalasi tongue.

Although the good news excited me, the word of Namiji's death cast dark shadows on my happiness. While Jim and I were in America, an epidemic of influenza struck Numba, and Namiji was one of several victims.

I remembered her kind loving face calling out to me on the way home from her garden. "Jaki, ese!" she'd call, and wait for me to appear at the kitchen window. I would find her holding out several long pieces of sugarcane, "I brought these for Ricky and Randy," she'd say, the warm smile never leaving her face.

Namiji was mother and grandmother to so many children not biologically her own. She even mothered orphan puppies, I remembered with a smile.

One afternoon as Chululu and I walked to the elementary school for a reading class, we passed the graveyard.

"My mother is buried here," Chululu informed me.

Remembering how viciously he reacted to his father's death, I shot him a glance to check his expression. There was no trace of anger on his face; God had transformed the fury into gentleness.

"We didn't wail for Wato after she died," he continued quickly. "Wato belonged to God. Now I'm waiting for the trumpet to sound, and when it does, I'm going to hook arms with her and go up to heaven—arm in arm."

Chululu's words set my heart pounding—*Namiji was a Christian when she died. I will see her again*. Another thing...I now knew Chululu had found the peace that defies death. The devil's stronghold was losing its grip.

Chululu chatted as we walked. He told me of the others who died with influenza at the same time. "A lot of wailing went on," he said, "but when they came to the house to wail for Wato, I told them to go someplace else and cry."

The words, "If any man be in Christ, he is a new creature," came to mind, and I realized I was walking beside one of God's miracles.

Chululu teaching a class at the elementary school.

Village life was not the same without Rick and Randy. The boys now lived at Ukarumpa attending school with other classmates whose parents lived in isolated villages. Rick lived in Dean Home with Stan and Carolyn Neher, caretakers of a home that housed twelve children. Randy, with a dozen other students, lived in Dorelo Home with house parents Cliff and Grace Dorn. The Nehers and the Dorns were dear friends, and leaving our sons at Ukarumpa was as comfortable as leaving them with family.

"When are Rick and Randy coming?" village friends asked almost daily, and we knew they missed our boys as much as we did. Talking to Rick and Randy on Sunday mornings by two-way radio helped the weeks fly by.

Jim and I gave thanks for the teachers who served God at Ukarumpa. Teaching was more than a job to them; it was a chosen commitment. God provided top quality servants to care for and teach our children. Some people might say we were depriving our boys of the education America offered, but we knew God provided Rick and Randy with the best of teachers and school experiences.

Chululu taught many people how to read.

One day as I was guiding Tanya through her correspondence lesson, a knock came at the door. A young man who had walked six hours over two mountains arrived to ask about having literacy classes in his village.

Later that evening, Chululu, Jim and I discussed the best way to reach the adults in those faraway villages. We decided that bringing in young men from each village, teaching them to read, then training them to teach their own people, would be the best way.

The decision required Jim and Chululu to take a motorbike trip to every village, check the interest in reading, and choose eligible men to become teachers. The survey trip would necessitate Jim's being gone at least one week.

A few days later, Jim gave Tanya and me good-bye hugs. Tanya and I walked outside onto the open porch as Jim drove around on the motorbike, reving the engine. Chululu climbed on the back of the bike and they were ready to go.

"Tell Jaki the speech you're going to give in each village," Jim prompted.

"No, no!" Chululu protested, hiding his face as if embarrassed. But with a little encouragement, he began: "If you come to class every day and aren't lazy, you will learn to read and write. Then, when you want to write a love letter, you won't have to ask someone else to write it for you. You can do it yourself and nobody will know...."

Remembering the love letter Taiva had received, we all laughed. It was a great sales pitch. Then, with the wave of hands, they were gone.

I picked up my four-year-old daughter and hugged her close. "Honey, it's just you and me now," I whispered. Long lashes framed her large brown eyes, as she looked back at me trustingly, not knowing her mother's limits. I thought about the generator I'd never started before, and feared we could very well be in the dark till Daddy came home again.

The best sound in the world to my ears was the hum of Jim's motorbike returning to Numba after being away five days. At first, Tanya didn't realize that the unshaven stranger who picked her up was her father; the beard made him unrecognizable. Jim carried the frightened child outside and set her in front of him on the motorbike. As he drove around the house, he sang their special "motorbike song," and the smile returned to her sunbronzed face.

Travelling with Chululu on motorbike to Managalasi villages.

"People were surprised to see us drive into their village," Jim reported to me afterwards. "We waited until everyone had gathered 'round before Chululu gave his speech. I wish you could have seen how excited they were. And when we left, all the villagers shouted and cheered. Almost everybody wants to learn to read."

Ten days later, twenty-four trainees arrived for the first teacher-training course. Since most of the students lived too far away to go home, Chululu assigned each one to a different home for the evening. The visitors noticed right away that the people who lived in Numba were different. They seemed happier, and there was no fear in their eyes. Instead, they wore big smiles on their faces and demonstrated relaxed attitudes. "We pray to God now, not to the spirits," their hosts would tell them proudly.

Each day began with either Poki or Chululu teaching from God's Word. The young men were reluctant to learn about Jesus, but after the first two days, they seemed to look forward to the devotionals even more than the training sessions; and after only one week, all but one of the trainees had accepted Christ as their personal Savior.

Chululu enthusiastically taught the training classes, preparing the new teachers for every problem he had previously encountered. Through the weeks of training, an evangelistic aura permeated Numba Village, like attending a Christian summer camp.

"It's so wonderful to live here and learn about God every day," one trainee remarked. Another said, "I don't want to return to my village, but just keep living here where I can listen to God's Talk (the Bible) until I die." Their words encouraged the believers and embarrassed the ones who still worshiped ancestral spirits.

After the course ended, the young believers expressed sadness and fear at having to leave the security of their environment and return to their villages. Jim assured them that he and

Chululu checking a new literacy teacher's class.

Chululu would visit once a week to supervise and assist; and, when their students had learned to read, Chululu would help them begin Bible studies.

Hallelujah! At last the privilege of reading and learning about God would reach out to include **all** the Managalasi villages.

The message we had waited months to hear finally came through. At precisely 6:30 AM the two-way radio blared from Ukarumpa: "Good morning, this is Mike Oscar. Today is Monday, April 17th, and I'm reading from Philippians 2."

I picked up my coffee cup and joined Jim on the couch. He sat clipping his fingernails, listening to the radio operator's selected reading. Then, using our call-sign, the operator said: "Sierra Oscar, I have traffic for you. Are you standing by?"

Jim reached for the receiver. "Roger, standing by."

"Good morning, Jim. Your Managalasi New Testaments arrived from Hong Kong over the weekend. The plane is on its way with 500 copies. Can you meet the pilot in about an hour and help him unload the Bibles?"

"I'll be there," Jim replied, still focusing on his nailclipper, but I knew his heart, like mine, was bursting with excitement.

Sonalu knelt on the porch blowing on embers, coaxing them to ignite so she could get a fire going. "Soso!" I called, and her head snapped up. "God's Book is coming on the plane today!"

"When?"

"Now! Jim's getting ready to go to the airstrip."

"Can I go with Jimmy?" she begged, grabbing my arm.

"Why don't you ask him?" I replied, noncommittally. "He's outside putting gas in the motorbike."

Sonalu leaped down from the front steps as Jim came riding around the house.

"Jimmy-o, can I go with you?" she pleaded, her face crumbling, like she was going to cry.

"I can't wait for you," Jim replied, laughing at her beseeching face, now a portrait of sorrow.

"Jimmy, please. If you don't take me with you, I'll die!" she blurted out, her mournful eyes never leaving Jim's face. Then, grabbing the handles of the bike, she fell to her knees and begged one more time. "Please, Jimmy!"

"Hurry! Quick! Hop on!" he commanded the woeful girl, and instantly her face changed from one of doom to ecstasy.

"Bring me a copy as fast as you can!" I yelled, waving goodbye. *What an actress!* I thought, smiling as I pictured Sonalu's woebegone face in my mind.

Tanya was in the yard playing hopscotch with her friend, Natalene. "Honey, come," I called softly, "it's time for your school lesson."

As I sat listening to Tanya read, my thoughts drifted back to the scene in front of the house. *Or...could seeing the New Testament really mean so much to Sonalu, that perhaps she wasn't "acting"?*

"The plane's coming!" Sonalu announced to Jim.

"Where? I don't see anything," Jim replied, scanning the horizon. Several seconds later, he, too, heard the buzz of the aircraft and followed the blue and white bird with his eyes as it careened in for a landing.

Sonalu stood to one side while Jim removed boxes and boxes of New Testaments from the belly of the aircraft. Finally, anticipation getting the best of him, Jim said, "I can't wait any longer," and tore open a box. He pulled out a single copy bound in dark blue vinyl. He stared at it for a moment; it looked beautiful. Anxiously, he opened the book and scanned each page.

Were the margins correct? Misspelled words? Pictures in the right places? He glanced up and caught Sonalu craning her neck, trying to see the book. "Can I hold one?" she asked.

"Of course," Jim replied, and handed her a book. As he reached for another copy, he noticed that Sonalu did not open the book; she just stood there holding it. Then, with closed eyes, she cradled the book to her chest and rocked it back and forth, as if it were a baby. "Thank you, Jesus, thank you, Jesus," she said, tears spilling over her cheeks.

Jim was startled for a moment. He tried to speak, but no words came. He reached out to touch her shoulder, but then drew back and touched his face, surprised to feel his own cheek wet with tears.

Jim continued to watch Sonalu hug her New Testament. In that moment, he felt the twelve years of concern and disappointments easing from his shoulders. This girl once worshiped ancestor spirits. The joy of seeing her now longing for God's Word made all the struggles worthwhile.

For twelve years, Jim and I had dreamed about this day... dedication day—the day that would climax years of learning the Managalasi language, cultural adjustments, translation and literacy. The steadily rising sun in a cloudless sky promised a perfect day for the fulfillment of this dream.

Jim and I rushed along the narrow trail from our house to the government station where the Managalasi New Testament dedication would take place. Our SIL aircraft buzzed overhead, shuttling in friends, officials and church dignitaries for the celebration.

Some of the Managalasi men who were to act as greeters painted their faces red and white and dressed in their most colorful feathers. "Oro! Oro!" they shouted, engulfing the visitors in a multitude of ear-splitting drum rolls as they stepped off the aircraft.

Many friends from Ukarumpa had taken the day to fly down and help us celebrate: couples who had taken care of our boys in the children's home, pilots who flew our supplies in every two weeks, teachers who taught our children, friends from the printshop who helped design and print our reading books, post office personnel who packaged up our mail and sent it to us in the village, secretaries and finance office personnel who kept records for us—all these friends had a part in helping us get the Bible translated into the Managalasi language. My heart surged with gratitude for each one.

The blue-covered New Testaments were piled in stacks on a table gleaming in the sun, taking the center of attention. After the opening prayer, Poki stood next to the table and spoke into a microphone. He told how he and Jim had struggled for words and concepts to put God's Word into Managalasi. Just before he sat down, he urged his people to buy a copy and to believe God's words.

Poki's voice did not tremble nor hint at the grief he felt inside. Had not word spread beforehand, no one would have suspected that Poki's five-month-old son Billy had been buried the day before, and now they witnessed him singing hymns of praise to God. According to Managalasi reasoning, no one could sing who carried heaviness in his heart for the loss of a child.

Murmurings spread among the crowd, but Poki pretended not to hear them. And the peace he demonstrated during this painful time made the words he spoke earlier come alive with meaning to all the unbelievers who sat in front of him.

After the last speaker sat down, Chululu stood to pray.

"Father, You could have left us in our sin, worshiping the spirits," he acknowledged to God, "but 'You thought of us for no reason' (grace) and 'You gave us Your heart' (love). You changed our lives and we became Your people...."

At the conclusion of the ceremony, Jim and I stood at the table prepared to sell the New Testaments. Men and women pressed around us wanting to exchange their one-kina coins (about one dollar) for a New Testament. The fragrance of the flowers that many had rubbed onto their bodies blended with the smell of the books.

"Jaki! Jaki!" someone called. I turned to find a gray-haired woman leaning over the table with her arm outstretched. She pressed her kina into the palm of my hand and waited for her book. The woman could not possibly have learned to read yet, so I reasoned she must be buying the book for someone else. I smiled in return and placed the New Testament into her hands, then watched to see what she would do. The woman ambled to a nearby tree and crouched on her haunches. She opened the book and rubbed her fingers lightly back and forth over the page. Her face seem to radiate as she turned pages, stroking each one lovingly. *The woman did buy the book for herself. She bought it just to hold, to touch.* I swallowed at the lump lodged in my throat.

I turned back to see many Managalasis holding God's Word in their hands for the first time, happiness visible on their faces. Surely, this must be a translator's dream come true.

The following Tuesday night, villagers crowded into the Meeting House with their New Testaments tucked proudly under their arms. Several who had openly opposed God squeezed in—carrying their Bibles like a flag of truce.

"Tonight, I'm going to teach about what happens to Christians when they die," Poki announced. "Turn in your Bibles to 1 Thessalonians, chapter four."

Those who had Bibles opened their books with confused looks on their faces and turned the pages randomly. They had no idea where to find 1 Thessalonians. Sonalu, Jim and I scrambled from person to person showing them where to look. The people sat so close together, it was hard not to step on someone. I made a mental note to begin teaching the women the books of the Bible, now that they could follow in their own Bibles.

When everyone found the text, Jim and I sat back and observed. Some people had their Bibles on their laps, others had theirs spread open on the floor in front of them. As Poki read aloud, they followed along with their fingers. Their faces glowed with emotion, and their smiles said, "This is real; now I know for sure that God is real."

My heart pounded like that multitude of drums on dedication day. This was the ultimate...to see people not only holding God's Word, but reading it with understanding and learning from it with joy on their faces. **This was the translator's dream come true.**

After the New Testament dedication, interest in learning to read spread like a fire out of control. Those who were literate met in the evenings and read Scripture together. Non-readers must have had a burning desire to read God's Book as hundreds enrolled in literacy classes. From these groups of readers small churches sprang up.

After being away at the center for over a year, Jim and I returned to Numba and noticed an air of excitement throughout the village. One by one, people approached us or visited at the house to tell us, "I'm all right now, I've got Jesus inside me." Then, in a tone that cautioned us, they added, "If you don't go to Bible study early, you won't get a seat."

Early? Jim and I looked at each other dubiously. In the nineteen years we lived at Numba, no one ever arrived "early" for any function.

On Thursday night, the biggest crowd ever gathered at Numba village meeting house. Even the windows were jammed with three and four people sitting in each one. Latecomers stood outside to listen.

Isai, Jim's first language helper, had never attended a Bible study before the dedication. Now he and his wife attended every service.

In one corner sat Marija, the village chief. For years Jim had pleaded with the chief to come and hear "God's talk," but Marija remained proud and aloof. Now, a soft countenance replaced the once hardened features of his face. "This is real," he told Jim. "Jesus lives in me, and I'm all right now."

Drums began to sound in a steady rhythm, and Aparihi, the songleader, led the group in singing. Then he announced he had written a new song, surprising both Jim and me. He taught the words first: "Thank you, Father, thank you, Father, thank you for sending Jesus to die for us." It was a simple hymn of praise, and we all learned the new song together. The melody was beautiful. I glanced at Jim as we sang. He sat there unashamedly letting the tears flow.

Sitting directly across from us, I noticed a strikingly handsome boy with light skin wearing a black T-shirt. *Who's that?* I wondered. *He doesn't look familiar. He must be from another village*. After singing a few more hymns, Aparihi called on "Morisi" to pray. When the black T-shirt stood up and began to pray, my heart leapt. This was the same person who saw Jim coming for Bible study and took off in the opposite direction. As Morisi prayed, I felt chagrined to think that even when I condemned him as "hopeless," God was loving him.

Later, as Chululu taught from the Word, I thought about the drastic change in Chululu's life after he became a Christian. *I'm so thankful, Lord, that even though I give up on people easily, You never do.*

Avovo, the spoiled child, grew up to be a straight-A student at the government school. Now he was preparing to go to Port Moresby to enroll in Bible school. Several others, both married and single, talked about doing the same.

I looked around the room filled with believers, their faces radiating God's light. At last these people were set free from their fears of ancestor spirits; God's Word had swallowed every ounce of darkness.

So why do I feel a tinge of sadness? I should be radiating joy and happiness along with them. Instead, I feel downcast and a little depressed. But why?

As I sat there trying to pinpoint the reason, the answer came to me. It was simple: The Managalasi people did not need us any longer. Everything we had helped them with—reading classes, training teachers, teaching the Word and writing hymns—they could handle on their own now. The people we had invested nineteen years of our lives in were indeed "all right now."

After Rick graduated from Ukarumpa High School, we flew as a family to Numba Village for the last time.

On our third night there, someone began wailing outside our bedroom window. Another joined him. But Numba people did not wail anymore. I poked Jim with my elbow. "Do you think someone died?"

"I'll go see what happened," he said, pushing the covers back. I got up and moved to the window.

"No, no one died," a man said to Jim. I recognized Isoro's voice. "It's because you and Jaki, Rick, Randy and Tanya are going. We feel sad, that is why we're crying."

Jim sat with them in the front yard for a while then came back to bed. The crying continued for a few hours, then silence. Thankfully, we slept. The next night several more came and wailed. "Jimi-oooo, Jaki-eyyyy," they cried, as if we had died. It was almost dawn before they returned to their houses. The wailing continued night after night.

One evening just before dark, two villages of people arrived dressed in new bark cloth, headdresses, beads and painted faces. "We came to dance all night for you," they said, shaking our hands in farewell. Jim and I stayed up to watch as long as we could. Then exhausted, we dropped into bed. It was easier to sleep to the sound of drums than to wailing.

We debated about what to do with our home. We had too many close relationships. If we gave our house to one of them, the others would be hurt. After much thought and discussion, we decided to dismantle the entire house, group the materials into five batches and give them to the five different clans. Each clan would then distribute the goods in their own way. No one would be left out.

One day as Jim was removing a window frame, a man arrived with his teenage daughter from a village on the other side of the government station. The girl's hand was tightly clasped in her father's. "I've come to give my daughter's hand in marriage to your son, Ricky," the man said. I felt my mouth drop open. I turned to see Jim's stunned look. My eyes flew back to the shy girl who stood by her dad's side looking at the ground.

When neither Jim nor I spoke, the father continued. "When you leave for America, leave Ricky here with us. He can marry my daughter, and she will take care of the gardens for him."

Jim finally found his tongue. "Rick can't get married yet, he's not finished with school," he explained. "After he graduates from college, he will decide where to live."

The man looked disappointed but seemed to understand. During our final week several more men wearing hopeful expressions approached us with their daughters in tow. Some came from Numba, some from other villages. We repeated the same to each man and watched the hope die on their faces.

Our last day arrived and the men went to the government station to purchase a cow; the women collected vegetables from their gardens; the older boys cut piles of sugarcane; and the girls gathered the brightest flowers to decorate the Meeting House. The younger children, along with Tanya, were running and jumping in a made-up game of their own. The village buzzed with activity, taking the edge off thoughts of our inevitable departure the next morning.

After the feast, we gathered in the Meeting House to say good-bye. Morisi was the first to speak. "You have given us something good," he said, addressing Jim and me, "but we have nothing good to give back to you, so we want you to have this." He reached for a coconut shell that sat behind him on a shelf. When he handed it to Jim, I saw it was filled with coins—a love gift from the believers. Overcome, neither Jim nor I could speak.

Chief Marija stood next, and immediately the room grew quiet. This man who had never spent a moment of his life in school had the aura of a president, maybe even a king. The chief stood there looking over the crowd, his eyes penetrating each person. Everyone waited respectfully for him to speak.

"Before you came," he said, swinging his eyes to Jim and me, "we prayed to the spirits. We were always afraid. And when our people died, we cried because we would never see them again. But now, because of Jesus, we don't have to be sad when our relatives die. We will see them again."

He had incredible authority in his gaze, and an uneasy feeling shot through me. I drew in a deep breath and waited.

"The villagers in American knew about Jesus for many, many gardens," the chief pointed out. "Why didn't your grandfathers come and tell our grandfathers? And your fathers come to tell our fathers? No one came to tell them, and now they all live in the fire."

I sat in numbed silence beside Jim as the chief returned to his place. When the quiet became awkward, Poki stood and talked about the early days when he was fearful of the "long man" with the large machete blade.

"My younger brothers would see the long man coming with his machete and hide in the bushes," he created a frightened look on his face, pretending to be one of the brothers. "Then, after Jim passed by, they would come out again." Soon the somber mood dissipated into laughter as the storyteller continued with several more stories.

Chululu was the last to speak. "You've been living with us for almost twenty years," he said. "Hundred of people have learned to read. We have a big church building and the New Testament that you translated."

"If we ignored the things you taught us and didn't believe in Christ, then you would have wasted these years, and your churches would have wasted their money.

"But the things you taught us have come good, and most of us are born again. And we're going to teach our children the new road, and our children will teach their children. We will all live in God's village together some day.

"When you go back to America, tell your friends that their money and their prayers have not been wasted. Tell your churches how thankful we are to them for sending you to give us God's Word. Tell them how it changed our lives and that we are now God's people."

"New Guinea! What a horrible place to live! Why do you want to change those people? They're happy as they are. And what about your children? Why are you going to deprive them of all America has to offer? Isn't that an incredible sacrifice to make for heathen people?"

The words of my former supervisor never quite left me over the nineteen years Jim and I lived among the Managalasis, but as I crossed the village for the last time on my way to the airstrip, I didn't see any "heathen" at all. Instead, I saw friends everywhere, their eyes puffy, lips quivering, faces distorted with sorrow. It was time to say good-bye. And it would be a long good-bye, for we would never meet again...on this earth.

I looked around at the world I loved, taking in impressions of the village, of the people, of the mountains, trying to store their images in my mind like a traveler storing food for a very long journey.

Chipi, now a young woman in her twenties, stood in front of her mother's house with an uncertain look on her face. She had been so quick to learn the syllables in our first reading class. I would never forget her smile of recognition and achievement when she put those syllables together and read words in her language for the first time. I wrapped my arms around her slender body and hugged her tightly, hoping to convey how much happiness she brought me, and how much I cared for her.

As I walked down toward the end of the village, I paused to stand in front of Ahmara's house. Before she died, she was the oldest Managalasi woman. Too old to get the fire going, I remembered how she would sit by the cold, gray ashes of her fire, rubbing her arms and stomach, trying to keep warm. *Because you believed in Him,* I said silently to the image of the old woman in my mind, *you will live forever.*

I reached the pathway that led away from the village, knowing that I was leaving Numba for the last time. I passed the graveyard where Namiji, my kindest friend, was buried. In my mind's eye, I saw the image of her warm smile and smudged face and spoke to the imaginary figure. *Even though you lived humbly, you'll stand beside the greats, like Billy Graham, and even the apostle Paul himself—because you believed.*

An incredible sacrifice for heathen people?

Yes, my friends, I addressed all the Managalasis, although none could hear me. *It was worth any sacrifice to bring you God's Word.*

At the airstrip, I felt the pressure of arms holding onto me. "You must come back to live with us again, to live with us and to die with us."

Chief Marija grasped my lower arm. He spoke slowly, calmly, but with great force. "All your children were born here," he said, pressing his fingers painfully into my flesh. "They learned to eat our food, speak our language, and do things the way we do them. They aren't Americans, they're Numba Village people! They belong to us!"

He became adamant as he held me with a penetrating gaze; I could not look away. "I've marked out a piece of my land for Rick and for Randy to make their gardens. I've put a taboo on the ground so no other person can plant food on their land. Your sons must come back here and marry Numba girls."

I felt my friends clinging to me, crying, calling our names in their wailing vibrato while the pilot waited patiently beside the small twin engine aircraft.

"Come on," Jim said, "we've got to take off while the weather holds. Help me get the boys into the plane!"

I looked around for Rick and Randy and spotted them entangled in a mass of arms that chained them to their friends. We tried to pry fingers away, but the grips grew stronger, the wailing louder. I gave up and climbed into the plane with Tanya. Jim and the pilot managed to free the boys from their beloved friends and we were strapped in our seats, ready for takeoff.

There was a loud sputter as the engines whirred to life, but then died out again. I held my breath, listening for the second start of the engines. There it was. And the rattling, shaking of the plane meant that we were moving to the top of the airstrip. The plane turned slowly, pausing before take-off. In those brief moments, I had one last glimpse of friends who would soon be treasured memories. They lingered beside the airstrip, staring back at us helplessly. Their broken faces tore my heart in two. Several young boys lay prone on the grass, their backs heaving up and down convulsively. The wheels of the Cessna rolled forward, and I caught Sonalu's eye above my crumpled handkerchief. The little smile she managed to give me hurt worse than the heartache behind my tears.

Within seconds, we were roaring down the slope of the mountain before lifting sharply. As we soared away from our Managalasi family, the pain in my body felt like the ache of influenza that works itself deep into the muscle, down to the bone.

Soon we would board a jet and be on our way to America.

America...where no one knocks at the door in the middle of the night asking for help, where the food is more to our liking, where the church services begin and end on time, where we can walk on paved sidewalks, where in the night we can exchange the sound of village drums for normal traffic noises.

A return to normalcy...is that what we wanted? Or could leaving this land possibly be *the incredible sacrifice?*